C000195126

THINK *like a* PHEASANT

Brian Mitchell

and the Rise of the Exmoor High Bird

THINK *like a* PHEASANT

Brian Mitchell
and the Rise of the Exmoor High Bird

BRIAN MITCHELL
with Stephen Manning

Quiller

First published in the UK in 2014
by Quiller, an imprint of Quiller Publishing Ltd
Reprinted in 2014

British Library Cataloguing-in-Publication Data
A catalogue record for this book is available from the British Library

ISBN 978 1 84689 200 4

Typeset by Arabella Ainslie
Edited by Kirsty Ennever

Printed in the UK by TJ International

Quiller
An imprint of Quiller Publishing Ltd
Wykey House, Wykey, Shrewsbury SY4 1JA
Tel: 01939 261616 Fax: 01939 261606
E-mail: info@quillerbooks.com
Website: www.quillerpublishing.com

Dedications

To my lovely devoted wife Angie, and my dear supportive friend, Alan Milton.

Brian Mitchell

To retired gamekeeper Sid Parris, who first introduced me to shooting and whom I blame for costing me a small fortune ever since.

Stephen Manning

Acknowledgement

Brian and Stephen would like to extend their sincere thanks to Prince Eric Sturdza and E.I.Sturdza Strategic Management Limited for their sponsorship of this publication

Photograph Credits

All photography by Charles Sainsbury-Plaice,
except for the following:

Becky Peat, *The Team*, page 7 colour plates
Becky Peat, *The Annual Boxing Day Shoot*, page 8 colour plates
Brian Mitchell, *Angie*, page 8 colour plates
Stephen Manning, front cover

CONTENTS

Preface		9
Introduction		11
1	The Morning After the Season Before	15
2	An Early Love of the Country	20
3	Mapperton – A New Life and a New Challenge	32
4	Miltons and the Goal of the Exmoor High Bird	40
5	Castle Hill – A New Beginning	73
6	'Prevention Better Than Cure…'	106
7	'Not Always the Most Popular Guy…'	137
8	The Future of the Exmoor High Bird	163
9	Legacy and the Future	185
Postscript		208
Index		211

A Beater's Poem to Brian Mitchell

A keeper rode into Castle Hill
Just twenty-five long years past,
His aim to build the greatest shoot
And really make a blast

He came with soul-mate Angie,
They called each other 'Hon'.
She worked with him so tirelessly
And it wasn't always fun!

He gathered a band of trusty chaps
And made his wishes plain.
His drive was unrelenting
And hell, didn't they groan with pain!

His tireless energy really worked
And brought such great success,
Although his band were on their knees
And poor Ange often stressed!

So, for all their loyal supporting,
And twenty-five years hard labour,
Surely Mitchell's troops deserve
Time off for good behaviour!

Gillian Tredgold, Castle Hill beater

PREFACE

I am extremely honoured and delighted to be asked to write a short preface to Brian Mitchell's book. Shooting is one of my greatest passions and I have been fortunate to have shot at some of the best shoots in the world. I am very privileged to be able to say that I have shot at Castle Hill for many years and I have witnessed first-hand the expertise and skill Brian Mitchell brings to the art – or is it a science? – of game-keeping.

I am sure that many readers of this book will have a love of shooting and I am equally sure that they will be able to recall the occasional uninspiring day, when things did not go as planned or the day did not meet their expectations. I have never experienced such a day at Castle Hill, for under the supervision of Head Keeper Brian Mitchell each drive is carefully considered. Wind direction, the amount of sunshine, atmospheric conditions, all these factors and more are carefully thought through by Brian to ensure that the best possible birds are presented to the guns. Again, I have shot at many superlative shoots, each of which is blessed with an inspiring Head Keeper but I can honestly and categorically say that Brian Mitchell is the Master. The superb quality of the birds Brian shows ensures that they are amongst the best in the world and because of this Castle Hill deservedly has an extremely high reputation. Of course the terrain is suitable for high birds, but this is just one factor in the success of Castle Hill and Brian's knowledge, skill and experience bring the best out of the wonderful Devon countryside.

This book is about more than just Castle Hill, for Brian has been instrumental in introducing the high bird to Exmoor. First at Miltons and then at several other shoots in the area, Brian has devised and supervised both shoots and drives to make the most of the deep valleys of Exmoor. He has been an inspiration to many keepers and his techniques and practices, although once thought of as unusual, are now viewed as common practice.

Brian has led a revolution in shooting and he has a legacy of which he can be proud: a legacy from which the sport will benefit for many years to come.

I am so pleased to be able to offer sponsorship of this book, via E.I. Sturdza Investment Funds. Brian has had a fascinating career and he has an important story to tell. I am honoured both to know Brian and to be able to shoot at Castle Hill.

I wish this book the greatest success.

Prince Eric Sturdza

INTRODUCTION

I first encountered Brian Mitchell some twenty-five years ago, when I worked on the Boconnoc Estate, near Lostwithiel in Cornwall. Surprisingly it was not shooting that brought us together, but Brian's other passion: cricket. Completely out of the blue, I received a phone call from Brian, who introduced himself and informed me that he was coming to Boconnoc to play cricket on the Estate's cricket pitch. Of course Brian's reputation from his years spent at Miltons was already well established and I certainly knew who he was, I just wasn't sure why he wanted to meet me! Of course I later discovered that the cricket match presented Brian with the perfect excuse to visit the Boconnoc shoot, for like any great enthusiast he will always take an opportunity to talk about his profession. Whilst Brian does have firm views on the art, or science, of game-keeping, he is also willing to listen and learn from others. Although we had never met before, I was soon persuaded to join him for dinner at the local pub. Over our meal and a few beers we picked each other's brains and thus began a friendship that has lasted to this day. Brian and his wife Angela have become very special friends to Amanda, my wife, and me. In the years since we have spent many happy days together at game fairs and various shooting related events all over the world, including two visits to the European Gamekeepers Association meeting in Austria. We have even been on holiday together.

Brian is a one-off character; a very special person of a type you meet very rarely in life. His enthusiasm for all things to do with the game-keeping profession is boundless and he is also one of the most competitive people I have ever met. To be frank, Brian can be an utter pain. Yet his unique drive and determination get things done and frequently win over doubting or reluctant minds. He never runs from a problem, but always tackles issues square on and for that alone he has long secured my respect and admiration.

Brian does not do things by halves and he is continually trying to improve the shoot to achieve perfection. Whatever Brian does, it is with huge enthusiasm and determination. He is a fantastic fundraiser having in the past, with the help of Maurice Pearce, raised many thousands of pounds for the game-keeping profession and continues to do so. I recall one year when we were on holiday in Portugal together, we spent the whole day, when we should have been relaxing, telephoning every keeper we knew to ask if they would pledge something for the sporting auction we were holding to raise funds for the National Gamekeepers' Organisation (NGO). Brian, in particular, was never going to take 'no' for an answer and the response we achieved was fantastic. With such great pledges the auction raised many thousands of pounds.

At some point Brian is going to have to slow down, but there are no signs that this is imminent. He is a tireless worker and passionate about the future of the game-keeping profession. Without his support, the NGO would not be in the position it is today – a respected organisation within the worlds of field sports and Government alike. Personally, he gave me enormous help in the early formation of the NGO and for that I will always grateful.

Brian's reputation within the West Country is legendary and many of the famous West Country shoots have used Brian as a role model, right from his early days at Miltons. His tireless work, and great success, at Castle Hill has ensured that his reputation has been even more enhanced. He is well-respected throughout the game-keeping world for his knowledge of game management and has on occasions been asked to give advice not only in this country but also abroad. At heart, Brian is a countryman, who loves nothing more than to be out and about looking after his beloved pheasants. Although his achievements at both Miltons and Castle Hill are substantial he is not one, as I have said, to rest on his laurels. He is such a grafter. His brain is never at peace, but is always thinking and looking to improve his birds, the drives and the shooting experience. He is a role model whom many gamekeepers would do well to follow. Brian has been at the forefront of many changes and innovations in shooting and I sincerely believe that much of what he has achieved or introduced will become standard practice across the game-keeping profession.

Brian has frequently told me that he is fortunate and privileged to have found a profession that has suited him so well and that has enabled him to give so much back. I, too, would say that I am fortunate and privileged to have worked alongside Brian and to consider him such a loyal and true friend. I know I can say, for both my wife and myself, that having Brian and Angie as such lovely friends has certainly enhanced our lives.

I wish this book great success. Not only is it an entertaining read, but much of the knowledge that Brian imparts will, I'm sure, be of assistance to those working in the countryside both now and in the future.

David Clark
Head Gamekeeper to Her Majesty The Queen,
The Sandringham Estate
Honorary President of the National Gamekeepers' Organisation

CHAPTER ONE

The Morning After the Season Before

The date of 2nd February is as significant and memorable to me as if it was my birthday or even Christmas Day. As a gamekeeper I have experienced nearly fifty such anniversaries and all follow the same initial pattern. As the morning light seeps in through the bedroom curtains, I am stirred awake by the pain that throbs through my temples, across my forehead and then envelops my whole body. Nearly all of us will have experienced that sort of pain at some point in our lives, but I know it is a feeling I will experience on every 2nd February, as long as I remain a gamekeeper.

The honourable profession of gamekeeping is not just a job, it is a vocation, a way of life, and is something I have been privileged to do, as I say, for close to fifty years. The last weeks of any season are always frantic as every available shooting day is taken up with syndicate days, bought days and the much-loved beaters' day. As the final day of the season is reached, on 1st February, there is still no time to reflect on what has gone, no time for a pat on the back, for there remains one last beaters' lunch, one last bowl of soup, one last drive and one final shot before it all comes to an end for another year.

For the past four months of the season I have been, it often seems, living in the pockets of the same good, reliable folk who have turned up on every shoot day, whatever the weather, to beat, pick up or load. I have an enormous amount of respect for them all. Sharing their company is a joy and I consider many of them to be firm friends, who have helped to keep me sane during the odd stressful moment when my best-laid plans didn't quite go to form. Their conversation, their humour and their passion for our sport is always a highlight of any season and it is truly a strange feeling of longing once the season is over, knowing that the intense relationship you have had with such colleagues is gone for another eight months. I must admit that I do feel rather lost when that final day is over. Yet there is still one more event to undertake before the season is over and that is the beaters' dinner. Even though I am often both physically and mentally exhausted by the rigours of the season, this last evening is never a ritual, never a chore, but a great opportunity to relax, unwind, thank many of my friends and colleagues and to have a beer, or two. Well, to be frank, it is always more than two and the evening frequently continues into the early hours of 2nd February... hence the pain on waking.

It is not just the hangover that has become a regular feature of the end of the season. Through the fog and pain I am able, at last, to collect my muddled thoughts on how successful the previous months have been. Despite all the planning and hard work, no season is the same and I must reflect on what have been the great successes, and the occasional disappointments, so as to learn how to improve the shoot for the following year. So whilst 2nd February is usually spent sitting in my kitchen in the company of a cup of black coffee and an aspirin, my brain is beginning to reflect and is already focusing on what needs to be done over the months ahead. On this day I find that I am, at best, physically weary, if not completely exhausted, but I still have to get out of the house to feed the surviving birds, even with a hangover!

Gamekeeping, and running a shoot day, is not an exact science and nothing is predictable. This in itself is exhausting both to the body and soul and certainly some seasons are harder than others. A very wet season, like that of 2012-13, may be beneficial in keeping the birds from wandering too far, but it introduces an additional pressure in that simply getting to feeders and moving guns and beaters around on shoot days can be extremely testing. A drier year, in which wild food is plentiful, often means that many hours are spent pushing the straying birds back towards the shoot. As I say, no season follows the same pattern as any other.

When I began my gamekeeping career, at the age of sixteen, what I lacked in experience and knowledge I certainly made up for in youthful enthusiasm. I did have the sense to listen and I rapidly learnt the secrets and necessities of my new trade from some very good teachers. Back then, a shoot day – during which I could walk a dozen miles or more, up and down valley sides – was taken in my young stride, as were the several pints of beer at the end of the day. Now, whilst I am still, thankfully, able to cover the miles, my body sometimes complains and, like most folk as they age, I have found that although I can still down the beers, the consequences are more severe. This is never truer than on those 2nd February mornings. Part of the ritual on these days is to kid myself that I really must avoid a hangover next time… yet surrounded by friends, with the great relief of knowing that the season has been a success, I am well aware that just one more beer will always seem like a good idea.

During the season, we at Castle Hill shoot four times a week; normally Monday, Tuesday and Friday, Saturday, which does not allow much time for 'normal' life to intrude. This work pattern, combined with the fact that during the last two weeks of the season I am out every day, results in something of a backlog of tasks. Once the season is complete I am soon hit with the realities of everyday life. In the months of the season, nothing else matters and tasks and responsibilities away from shooting are placed very much on the back-burner. Whether it is household chores, catching-up with non-shooting friends and family, servicing vehicles, decorating the house, even talking to my wife, Angie, about non-shooting things, all suddenly become of paramount importance. It is almost as if I lead two completely separate lives and for a period of a few weeks, before once again my gamekeeping life takes over, I live a comfortable, if hectic, 'normal' existence. It is during these weeks that my wife and I manage to grab a week or two away. Having just spent the last months at the mercy of the elements, I long to escape from the Devon mud, wind, rain and, occasionally, snow, to a warm sunny climate and for a few days at least I allow the stresses and strains of the previous months to ease from my body as I become a sun worshipper.

Yet for all its pressures, work to me is a holiday, one that I have been privileged to enjoy for nearly fifty years. Even as I relax on a poolside lounger, my thoughts soon stray to what needs to be done on my return to prepare for next season and it doesn't take me long to compile a comprehensive list. I am extremely fortunate in that I am now supported by three beat-keepers and one under-keeper at Castle Hill, who relieve me from many of the early pressures. Whether it is repairs to pens, improving paths and tracks or catching last season's old birds to send them off to the game farm, all are tough physical tasks and it is reassuring to know that I have an excellent, reliable team to help me with them.

Then of course there is the forward planning for the next season: much of this centres on which cover crops to plant and where, as well as considering the long-term development of the shoot. These thoughts may be of new drives, or variations to existing ones, or the planting of more permanent cover crops, such as laurels.

At Castle Hill we have, and will continue, to focus on conservation and much of this has focused on the planting of woodlands. Oak, hazel and beech trees have been planted, not only to provide cover and shelter for the game birds, but also to encourage other flora and fauna. The reputation of the Castle Hill shoot is not one that has been easily won and I for one am very conscious that it is a reputation that not only needs to be maintained but enhanced. If you are not moving forward as a shoot, you are moving backwards. The guns who shoot at Castle Hill demand high, challenging birds and expect variation. I see one of my biggest duties as Head Keeper is to progress the shoot and ensure that none of us involved with the running of it become complacent. Legacy is also very important to me and I love to think that the work we are doing now at Castle Hill will benefit future guns, in perhaps thirty or more years' time.

I suppose I have a firm philosophy about gamekeeping and shooting that will become apparent throughout this book. I certainly like to think that I am professional in my work and I would be the first to admit that this professionalism is driven by my personal obsession to get things right. This, I imagine, is an intrinsic part of my DNA, my make-up, but I also like to think much of my success can be firmly laid at the feet of those for whom I have been privileged to work, as well as those I have worked alongside who have taught and shown me the ways of gamekeeping.

CHAPTER TWO

An Early Love of the Country

The year 1948 was an Olympic year, with the games held in a bomb-scarred London. It was also the year I was born, the youngest of two children, my sister, Brenda, having arrived two years earlier. I grew up in the village of Milborne Port on the Somerset-Dorset border. My father, Stanley, was the Head Gardener at a large country house, Ven House. He was a very strict father and if ever I misbehaved I would incur his wrath, but I had total respect for him. We lived in the old gamekeeper's cottage, attached to the Estate. My childhood was spent surrounded by, and in, the countryside and it must have been in these early years that I acquired my love and respect of all things country. My father kept bees, harvested and sold the honey, grew fruit and vegetables for the family table, with some to spare, and his pride and joy was the cultivation of carnations which, much to his delight, frequently won prizes at our annual village flower and produce show.

There is no doubt that my father encouraged an understanding of nature and this was no more true than on our regular family Sunday walks, which we enjoyed after one of my mother's wonderful lunches. Folk were just so much more connected to the countryside then, whether for work or the fact that they were surrounded by it, than we are today. Fruit and vegetables were, unlike today, strictly seasonal and I can still recall my mother's delicious puddings produced from whatever was in season. I always enjoyed the first peas or runner beans from the garden and the flavour of English strawberries, eaten when they were perfectly ripe, was simply magical. Our Sunday outings are one of the few memories of time spent with both my mother and father during my childhood for, like many families, my parents worked extremely hard to feed and clothe us. Whilst my father supplemented his wages with produce from our garden, as well as the honey, my mother, Lilly, was an out-worker for the Ensor glove-making business, which was based in Milborne Port, and she would spend hours in our smoke-filled kitchen stitching gloves. Indeed it sometimes seemed that this task took over her life and I do recall that she would sometimes work for days on end to complete a large order. Tragically, my mother died of cancer when I was just fourteen, a victim of her devotion to Senior Service cigarettes. My mother's death gave me a lifelong hatred of smoking and a firm determination never to do it myself.

My parents introduced my sister and me to the flowers of the hedgerows and to the seasons. Although these are wonderful memories they are tinged with sadness, for not only were they brief moments in my life but these Sunday walks also coincided with the outbreak of myxomatosis amongst the rabbit population. In my mind's eye I can still clearly see images of the suffering this dreadful disease inflicted upon those unfortunate animals. I am convinced that the consequences were significantly more far-reaching than just the horrors the rabbits had to endure. Before the onset of the myxomatosis outbreak, rabbit meat was a staple food not only for rural folk but also for city dwellers; just twenty-five years ago two gentlemen earned a living at the Castle Hill Estate as rabbit trappers. Smaller pheasant shoots would often subsidise their running costs by trapping rabbits. For example, at the Woolland shoot in Dorset, right into the late 1950s, numbers in excess of 20,000 were caught over a season. Both the fur and the meat found a ready market and caught rabbits would be sent to the London markets by train. In addition, the demise of the rabbit has forced other animals – such as foxes, buzzards and sparrowhawks – to look elsewhere for their sustenance and I am convinced that this is why the grey partridge has disappeared from the West Country, along with much of the songbird population.

Although I was a keen learner when it came to matters of the great outdoors, the same cannot be said about my school work. The first school I attended was the local village school in Milborne Port before moving on to King Arthur's School, about nine miles away in Wincanton. My teachers must have despaired of me, for I simply did not want to be imprisoned in a classroom when the exciting world of the countryside was just waiting for me to explore it. Of course no one then had even heard the word dyslexia, let alone knew what it meant; one legacy of this is that I am the most appalling speller, though this has not really held me back in my chosen career. Whilst good at most sports, including the trampoline, academically I did not flourish, for I spent too much classroom time staring out of the window, dreaming of what I could see and learn from the countryside.

I think that I was something of an embarrassment to my perfect sister, who was always an A-stream pupil, whilst I, with my dirty knees and filthy fingernails, was always destined to spend my life out of doors. One advantage for her of having such a brother was that I offered no resistance when it came to choosing our bedrooms. When we moved to a new Estate dwelling at West Lodge, I wanted the small box-room, which overlooked a wood at the back of our house and from which I could watch the comings and goings of the local wildlife, whilst Brenda was very happy to get the larger bedroom. At least that was one thing we did not argue over!

I was extremely fortunate that, apart from my parents, a local farmer, Ron Knight, took me under his wing. Of course my mother's death left a huge void in my life, which my outings with Ron helped to fill. I spent many a happy hour in his company, perhaps lamping foxes or shooting rabbits, or just listening to what Ron had to say about the ways of the countryside.

Ron owned an antique, bolt-action .410 shotgun, which he never locked away, and it was always lying around his dairy. It seemed to be lubricated with tractor engine oil, for it was always filthy, but I loved it. After several months of pestering poor old Ron, he finally admitted defeat and allowed me to fire his precious gun. Once he had taught me the basics of gun safety I was privileged enough to be allowed to walk the hedges around the village and secure the odd rabbit for the family table.

Ron was also the person who introduced me to the fun of 'squirrel poking' as a means of pest control. We first went into nearby Hanover Wood and, armed with a long aluminium pole and our shotguns, we would poke the squirrel drays with the pole. This would encourage the squirrels to bolt from the safety of their homes and we then had the excitement of trying to shoot the speeding squirrels as they jumped from branch to branch. Not only was this method vital as a means to control the ever-increasing grey squirrel numbers – vermin that can do so much damage on a shoot – but it also improved our shooting and the speed of our reactions, for squirrels can certainly shift when they need to. On several afternoons Ron and I shot eighty or more squirrels from just one wood.

It was around this time, when I was fifteen, that I snared my first fox, also in Hanover Wood. This was rather naughty of me as the ground at that time was very much the domain of the local hunt, whose members would not have been best pleased to learn that I was reducing their sport. However, I was young and very keen, and I did not always think of the consequences of actions.

A few weeks later I was able to help the local Blackmoor Vale Hunt when, as I was out watching them galloping across the fields near Milborne Port, I saw their quarry seek refuge in a mass of bushes. I rushed over and turned out the fox, pushing it back towards the hounds, who duly claimed it. The Master, following country tradition, presented me with one of the fox's paws in recognition of my assistance. I was as proud as Punch to have been so honoured and took the trophy to school to show to my friends. However, with the ever-wandering mind of a fifteen-year-old, I promptly forgot that I had left the paw in my school desk. There it remained for the whole of the summer break and on our return to school in the autumn, the stench in the classroom was something to experience! The paw was green and full of maggots and it took several weeks for the appalling smell to leave the building. I was not popular amongst either staff or pupils for this little oversight.

To illustrate how the countryside has altered, I need go no further than recollect one of my many shooting experiences with Ron: driving out in the twilight, on the back of a very ancient tractor, for an evening of lamping foxes, we came across a covey of grey partridge resting in a field. Ron, without a second's hesitation, raised his shotgun and claimed two birds for the pot. Such behaviour was not frowned upon then, for it was accepted that food could be obtained for the table in this manner and the grey partridge, now very rarely seen in the West Country, was so common in the late 1950s.

Ron not only taught me how to shoot safely, but he also introduced me to my future career when, during the shooting season, he would take me every Tuesday to the local shoot at Woolland, where Arthur Henstridge was the Head Keeper. Arthur was a legend amongst the gamekeeping fraternity and here my ability to listen quietly and to learn was invaluable. To be fair, my school teachers never raised a complaint about me missing lessons on shoot days, when I would be in the beating line, and I can only assume that this was because they realised where my heart lay.

I met my first girlfriend, Joyce, at King Arthur's. We were both aged fifteen and still yet to experience our first kiss. I managed to orchestrate a walk into the countryside and we settled down in a field for an innocent moment. During this encounter I too, rather like my teachers, realised exactly where my true interests lay – for as Joyce and I were exchanging a kiss, I looked over her shoulder and was more taken by the wonderful wild flowers, insects, butterflies and birds that were all around us than the new activity in which I was engaged! On a serious note, the fields of my youth have disappeared to simple grass, which has had a devastating effect on the flora and fauna of the British countryside. Wild flower meadows are now a very rare sight and their demise has resulted in a dramatic decline in insect and butterfly numbers and I am sure this has had a big impact on the songbird population. This is something we have tried to address at Castle Hill, but more of that later.

The death of my mother had a practical consequence too, in that my sister and I moved to Sherborne in Dorset to live with my aunt, my father's twin sister. Although my father had tried to raise us himself, he found that with the long hours on the Estate he simply could not be around enough at home. Once school was behind me, I started to look for employment. I was determined that this had to be of the outdoor variety and I fortunately heard via the local jungle-drums that the shoot attached to the Sherborne Castle Estate was looking for a trainee gamekeeper. Nervously I applied for the position, and to my huge disappointment I did not get it. Fortunately, however, I must have impressed somebody. After just a few months in the role, the young lad who had been successful decided that the gamekeeping life was not for him. I was contacted by the Head Keeper, a gentleman by the name of Ron Day, who offered me the job: I raced up to his house at top speed on my BSA Bantam to accept it.

The only word I can use to describe my first season is 'magical' – for I quickly realised that the gamekeeping life was one hundred per cent for me. I felt completely at home in my chosen profession, despite the long and demanding hours which would sometimes see me tearing around on my elderly motorbike in the dark at five a.m. I loved the challenges imposed by nature and the birds which made, and continue to make, every day and season different. To modern keepers the methods that I first learnt may seem antiquated. We did not have the luxury of incubators, but utilised a rearing field in which pheasant eggs would be hatched by broody hens, which would be supplied by local farmers. This in itself was quite a science. We would have to make a nest of hay in a hatching box, in which dummy eggs were placed. Once the hens had the right idea, we would place between fifteen and twenty pheasant eggs in the hatching box and let nature take its course. This approach was extremely labour-intensive and involved long hours, especially once the eggs began to hatch. Once the poults were ready to be transferred to the pen we would let them go back into the hatching box at night and cover this with sacking, thus trapping the birds. At first light, box, hen and poults would then be manhandled to a quiet woodland clearing and allowed to gentle and gradually find their way out to their new home.

Work sometimes got in the way of pleasure for I was a keen cricketer yet, even on a Sunday afternoon when I was due to play for the local team, the birds had to come first. On one particularly sunny Sunday I was about to disappear in the direction of the pitch when I was firmly told by Ron that I could not go until the birds had been watered. This job usually took some time, but I was so desperate to play cricket that I picked up a watering can in each hand and literally ran up and down the pens, refilling the cans with water as necessary, and ensured that the task was completed in record time. I arrived at the cricket ground just in time for the start of the match, soaked and breathless!

I was helped in my task by a retired policeman named

Charlie Carter, who on cold mornings would brighten my day by bringing me a hot cup of Camp Coffee. Once the eggs hatched, the chicks would be moved to a feeding pen where they would be fed on Crumbs feed. The feed bags would be fastened with string and I remember Charlie would take this string home for his wife to use around the house, for repairing socks and the like, so in true country fashion, nothing was wasted!

Charlie was the proud owner of an ancient 12 bore hammer gun that he polished constantly, so much so that the barrels shone in the sunlight. Knowing of my passion for shooting, he very kindly gave me the gun to use. However, I soon discovered that any intended prey, such as crows or pigeons, easily spotted the very shiny barrels. So I had what now seems like a very silly idea – I painted those stunning barrels with matt black paint. Although this improved my shooting, the look on Charlie's face when I handed back his precious gun to him was one of total dismay. I understand that it took him hours and hours to strip off the paint and restore the gun to its former glory!

Charlie and I, along with his grandson John Head, would occasionally go squirrel hunting. I was always keen to be the one to poke the dray and when doing so I would lean my gun against a tree. I later learnt that John or Charlie would take the cartridges out of it, so that when I rushed to pull the trigger on the fleeing squirrels I would hear the ominous click of an empty gun. I assumed at the time that I had inexplicably failed to load the gun and it took me some time to work out what was going on…

There were two shoots on the Estate, Deer Park Side under the control of Ron Day and Honeycombe, which was run by John Yandle, and it was with John that I gained my first year's experience. In my second year John Turner was brought in to oversee the shoots, and I would float between the two whenever and wherever I was needed. Both shoots at this time put down around 1,000 birds, which with the use of broody hens, and later incubators, meant that I was always busy. John Turner was renowned for having something of a temper and I came to experience this on more than one occasion. In my youthful enthusiasm I had decided to act independently to solve an ever-increasing fox problem and I set two snare traps along a well-known fox route. Unfortunately, the following day the shoot owner's daughter was a walking gun during one of the drives and managed to catch herself twice on these snares. I was soon hauled up in front of John and experienced one of his infamous bollockings, which left me in tears.

It was not just John whom I upset with my youthful enthusiasm. I was always ready for a joke, a tendency that occasionally verged on cockiness. The Sherborne shoot possessed a rich collection of characters in both the beating line and amongst the pickers-up. One such gentleman was a local farmer by the name of Ernie Swain, a huge and rather rough man, who suffered from a bad limp. Ernie was utterly dependable and first-rate at his job as a picker-up. I cannot even remember what I said to annoy Ernie, but I must have been cheeky or just downright rude to him, which he was not going to accept from a sixteen-year-old pipsqueak. Whatever I said, my timing was poor, for Ernie had just retrieved a shot mallard and he used the carcase as a weapon with which to hit me on the side of the head. The blow certainly hurt, but I think I was more shocked than anything. I did, however, learn a valuable lesson on how to address people – or at least how not to.

Whilst at work, I was always looking for ways to save time. One of the most laborious jobs was the transfer of the newly hatched birds from the hatching boxes to their feeding pens. This involved carrying the broody hens, one at a time, to the new pens, a distance of several hundred yards. The newly hatched birds would be boxed-up and I would carry the hen under one arm and the box under the other. This was surprisingly hard physical work and very time-consuming. I considered that if I placed the broody hen on the ground and carried the noisy chicks in the box, the hen would follow the sound and reduce my load. Although the transfer was successful, the hens were upset by this undignified approach and refused, at first, to have anything to do with the young birds. For this experiment I received yet another dressing-down! On another occasion, again acting independently, I decided to leave a trail of corn through a wood to entice the pheasants on to a drive. However, my endeavours only succeeding in leading the birds in the opposite direction and once again I was up in front of John and his temper. Despite these youthful mishaps, and I am sure there were many others, John and Ron clearly saw that I possessed the desire and willingness to succeed.

However, this desire did not stop me from getting into difficulties. Behind Sherborne Castle lies a fifty-acre lake, which in the mid-1960s was very overgrown with weed. In early September each year the lake was the scene for a wild duck shoot. Although no duck were ever put down, the amount of weed in the water attracted literally hundreds of them. As the lowest of the low under-keepers, I was given the thankless task of rowing one of the guns, Admiral Best, out into the lake to a small island in the middle where a hide was placed in which to await the flight of the ducks. To this day I don't know exactly how the boat began to take on water; I think it might have been the fact I was so keen to get on to dry land that I rowed too fast. Of course the more water that came in-board, the faster I rowed. As you can imagine, the Admiral had quite a lot to say about my seamanship, which only panicked me further. We were able to get within a few yards of the island before the boat finally succumbed to its watery grave. The Admiral did not go down with his ship but, cursing me and the predicament we found ourselves in, we clambered onto dry land holding two shotguns above our heads. I am sure that the scene must have caused much controlled laughter from those watching us on shore and a boat was duly sent to rescue us. I was never allowed to forget my first – and last – rowing expedition.

Towards the end of my third season at Sherborne I was given the honour of being able to carry my gun at one of the last shoots and it was then that I claimed my first ever pheasant. Unlike today, when the beaters' day shoot is an accepted, almost expected, perk for those who have helped make the season a success, then it was a real privilege to be asked to shoot, as pheasant numbers were so much lower than the thousands that many shoots now release. I can recall that I was allowed to stand on just one drive and I managed to shoot the one cock bird that came my way. To my delight, and perhaps surprise, it folded in the sky and fell to the ground, stone dead. There was a sense of achievement and satisfaction that I had made my first pheasant kill and perhaps a little youthful arrogance that it appeared to be so easy. Naturally this feeling diminished quite quickly over the years when I discovered that I could miss just as easily as everyone else!

One other shooting memory from my time at Sherborne was the annual cull of the four hundred or so fallow deer that were kept in the park next to Sherborne Castle. Each year around forty to fifty deer would be culled so as to keep numbers stable and the herd disease-free. I took some pleasure in watching Ron Day shooting, but I didn't enjoy the consequences, for although we had a ready market for the venison, the offal had to be disposed of and, as the youngest employee, this rather distasteful and smelly job fell to me. I had to dig a trench and, once the deer were cleaned, it was my task to throw the innards into the hole. On one occasion Ron decided to play a practical joke on me and, when I was distracted by my unpleasant work, he managed to slip two deer testicles into my jacket pocket. At this time I was lodging with my aunt and I returned home that day completely unaware of what was lurking in my clothing. Of course this was the one day that Auntie decided to hang up my jacket and I can still hear her screams as she discovered the 'presents' Ron had left for me.

Isolating the deer to be culled was never easy. It fell to me to drive a rather old Land Rover towards the herd in an attempt to separate the animals. I have always been a rather speedy driver and the faster I drove, the faster the deer ran. Ron was in the back of the open-top vehicle and the more I gathered speed, the more he was bounced around, until finally my driving literally bounced him out of the back. After three rather undignified bounces he finally stopped, with the barrel of his rifle firmly embedded in the ground next to him. Ron was rather bruised, the rifle was amazingly undamaged, but again I received a good telling-off, which was made worse due to the fact that I could not stop laughing!

In the summer of 1967, after three seasons at Sherborne, I was approached by Victor Montagu, (Earl of Sandwich), to see if I would be willing to accept the gamekeeper/estate manager position on the Mapperton Estate in Dorset. This would involve looking after the shoot, which at that time was run solely for the enjoyment of the Montagu family and their friends, as well as some forestry work. My father, who had initially tried to persuade me away from a gamekeeping career, for he thought that there was no long-term future in it, drove me to Mapperton to meet the Earl and view the Estate.

CHAPTER THREE

Mapperton – A New Life and a New Challenge

I met my first wife, Sally, whilst at Sherborne and I am convinced that our first child was conceived on the joyful night that England beat West Germany in the World Cup final of 1966. I remember that it was one hell of a party! When my father discovered that Sally was pregnant he marched us both off to see our local vicar and within weeks we were married. So the Earl of Sandwich's offer came just at the right moment, for our son Simon had recently arrived and I was delighted to accept a new job that was a step up the ladder. In my first season, I reared 300 pheasant and fifty duck and I remember that these numbers seemed more than enough for a then nineteen-year-old keeper to manage.

My new position came with a pay rise and a cottage, but Sally and I did struggle to make ends meet in our early years together. To supplement my income I would grow my own vegetables, catch and skin rabbits and snare foxes. These I would also skin and nail the pelts to an old door, which I would then bring into the living room so as to dry them out by the fire. The smell was disgusting, but the money I received for the fox hides certainly helped to keep our heads above water.

Moving to a new part of the country was a somewhat daunting experience for Sally and me, young as we were, but the process was made much easier by the warm welcome we received from the locals, in particular George Brown, his wife Bobby and their family. George was a tenant farmer, running a farm that was adjacent to the Mapperton Estate, and he had run the shoot for a number of years before my arrival.

George used to organise one or two larger days a season at Mapperton for family and friends of the Montagu family, as well as a number of rough, walked-up days, and would later shoot with Alan Milton and his team. George was free with his helpful advice as well as his company and I would regularly descend upon his farmhouse for a cup of tea and a chat after my early morning rounds. Although the farmhouse kitchen was always warm and welcoming, the same could not be said for George's collie which, for some reason, took an instant dislike to me. Normally a placid animal, on sight of me it would hide under the kitchen table, only to emerge, as quick as a flash, to try and take a bite out of me, before retreating to her sanctuary once more. On a number of occasions the damn dog was successful and succeeded in sinking her teeth into my seat. Running repairs were carried out by George's wife, for she could not bear to see me going out with rips in my trousers. I must have looked a funny sight, sitting in the kitchen, mug of tea in hand, chatting away without any trousers on. Despite that dreadful dog I have very happy memories of my early morning cuppas with George.

As the likes of Ron Knight and others had encouraged my interest in gamekeeping, so I have always tried to encourage others to appreciate and gain an understanding of the countryside. When I first arrived at Mapperton I was fortunate to make the acquaintance of three local twelve-year-olds: Nigel Brown, George's son, Henry Buckmaster and Giles Wood, all of whom were as keen as mustard to help out on the shoot and assist me with vermin control. The three soon joined the beating line and most nights one or more of them would join me as I sped around the Estate in search of rabbits, foxes, magpies and other pests. I am very pleased to be able to say that all have remained in contact and have some link to the countryside to this day, whether it be for work or pleasure. Giles boarded at Eton and came home to Mapperton during the holidays. He was an able beater and I always enjoyed introducing Giles to the guns as my 'Eton beater'. On a non-shoot day Giles always took the opportunity to have a lie-in and would frequently arrive at our house just as we were stopping for lunch so he could get his breakfast!

My Estate vehicle was a Mini Cooper pick-up, which I would fling around the local lanes and the Estate. I have always been a person in a hurry and never more so in or on a motor vehicle. I turned this lovely car over on a couple of occasions in my haste to get from A to B. Once I even turned the vehicle on to its side, it continued to roll over and went on to its roof, with me hanging upside-down inside, then tipped back on to its other side and finally righted itself on to its four wheels. All this happened with the engine still running and as soon as the wheels touched the ground once more, I simply continued my journey!

I know I have gained something of a reputation over the years for my somewhat erratic driving and have had more than my fair share of driving 'incidents', mostly explained by the fact that I am constantly rushing around. My time at Mapperton provided no respite from a catalogue of motoring-related accidents. One night I was out lamping foxes with Nigel Brown, who was in the open back of the Mini Cooper pick-up. We saw a fox and I floored the accelerator in hot pursuit of our fleeing prey. As I sped uphill across a field, the low clearance of the Mini caused the vehicle to be grounded on a raised mound. The result was that from travelling at a speed in excess of thirty mph we stopped dead in a split-second and the momentum flung poor Nigel out over the bonnet of the car, sending him crashing into the hillside. Fortunately, apart from a few bruises, he was unhurt. On another occasion, again whilst I was pursuing a fox, this time it was Giles who was thrown out of the back of the Mini, when I took a very sudden ninety-degree turn. Again, my companion was unhurt but the 12 bore Holland & Holland side-by-side shotgun that Giles had borrowed from Victor Montagu had had its stock snapped in two. Naturally I was mortified but luckily for me the gun's owner was very gracious when he saw the results of my driving!

Despite being someone who has spent his life around dogs, I would be the first to confess that I am useless with them, especially gundogs, which is something of an admission for a gamekeeper. I seem to have a natural ability to ruin even the best trained dog and I now have the sense to leave all the dog work to my second wife Angie, who is a complete natural with them. My gundog experience can be summed up with a tale from my time at Mapperton. One summer I went along to the Cattistock County Fair where a well-known golden retriever breeder, June Atkins, ran a trial. Two gamekeeping friends persuaded me that just for fun we should enter one of these gundog trials, which involved the throwing of a dummy for our dogs to seek and retrieve. My two mates went first, and they and their dogs successfully impressed both June and the large crowd that had gathered to watch. When my turn came I duly sent out my curiously named dog, Honey – for she was black – a collie-labrador cross. Honey went halfway towards the dummy but then decided that a nearby hedge offered more in the way of entertainment and charged into it, bolting a rabbit in the process. Now there was nothing Honey liked more than to chase a rabbit, and, despite my shouts, she chased after her prey at full-tilt. The rabbit proceeded to run right through the fairground, with both Honey and me in hot pursuit. The roars of laughter from the crowd followed me and brought a swift end to my attempts to enter the world of trialling. Honey and I came a poor third out of the three competitors.

I found that I thrived in my new position at Mapperton: being in sole charge suited me. Although I was still very much a young man with a great deal to learn and mistakes to make, I had the necessary passion, commitment and confidence to do the job. I was given free reign to introduce new drives and steadily increased the number of birds put down. A few hundred soon became nearly a thousand and within four years, whilst Mapperton still remained a family shoot, we were putting down around 2,000 birds. By the end of my time there the shoot started the season with 8,000 pheasants. In the early 1970s this was a very significant figure, which, shooting once a week, meant that we confidently achieved days of 250 birds or more.

I quickly realised that the future development and success of the shoot depended on active vermin control, the use of cover crops (although this was fairly limited at first) and the development of the three main woodland areas on the shoot. As many will know, it is vital that pheasants feel that they have somewhere warm and sheltered to which to return, with plentiful food and water, to stop the birds from wandering. In particular, the sites of Home and Burcombe Wood provided these requirements. With the careful placement of sewelling, these two drives allowed me to produce some reasonably high birds, although not to the same heights as on Exmoor.

Apart from my reliable young beaters and some enthusiastic locals, I was quickly able to acquire the help of a great beating team that was led by my beat-keeper, Keith Grintow, who was even younger than me. I suppose Keith was the first person I had to manage, in effect, and I am sure he probably cursed me on certain days, especially when the day was not running quite as planned and he bore the brunt of my temper. Having said that, if we ever had a cross word I would always ensure that we moved on from it quickly. I know I was a hard taskmaster to Keith, for if I gave him a job to do I expected it to be done. This is not to say that there were not a lot of laughs in our relationship. For example when we stopped for a break and a cup of tea, I was always in such a hurry to get on that I would down the scalding hot liquid before Keith had even considered raising his cup to his lips. In an attempt to slow me down one day, Keith put salt instead of sugar in my tea and this did make me take a few extra minutes that day! I got my revenge, sort of, when he came to load at Miltons a few years later and I put salt in the cup of tea I handed him. He must have been suspicious, but, much to my disappointment, managed to drink the tea without outwardly showing any reaction! Keith also had the annoying habit of smoking and whenever I could I would grab his cigarettes from him, whether singly or in packets, and throw them out of our speeding shoot vehicle. Sadly I was never able to persuade him to give up the evil weed.

Mapperton, like many Estates, is bordered by farms whose owners frequently put down a number of birds themselves for their own pleasure. Such action does nothing to ease the problem of birds straying on to other shoots and at Mapperton we did suffer from this. It was not unknown for certain individuals even to encourage the movement of birds on to their land and I did get rather upset by this. As I have matured I have learnt that as long as folk are not too blatant, it is an aspect of managing a shoot that must simply be accepted. You have to live and work alongside your neighbours and the best way to achieve harmony is through mutual respect, a smile and a handshake. After an incident at Mapperton that did not go well, I learnt to avoid confrontation as much as humanly possible and this approach stood me in good stead when I moved to Exmoor.

From 1970 onwards we began to let some commercial days, mainly to a company called Game Finders, which was run by a gentleman called Chris Oliver. (He, wearing another hat, worked for Fountain Forestry.) Game Finders specialised in letting deerstalking days, mainly to continentals, but Chris was keen to diversify into driven game shooting. With the Montagu family now reluctant to put any more investment into the shoot to raise it up to the next commercial level, when I was approached by Chris to see if I would be happy to be directly employed by Game Finders, on the Montagu land, I gladly accepted. I considered that I still had plenty to give the Mapperton shoot as well.

Now being part of the world of commercial shooting presented new challenges, but great pleasures as well in that I had the opportunity to meet new, interesting and very affable folk. One such person was Alan Milton, who led a roving syndicate of guns from Barnstaple that shot throughout the west of England. From 1970 onwards, Alan and his team would regularly make two or three appearances at Mapperton every season, buying days from Game Finders, and I am sure that they enjoyed their time and liked what they saw. I prided myself that if a team had booked and paid for a 200-bird day, or whatever the figure was, I would give them that amount and would avoid any sort of 'bag-filling drives'. Birds would be presented that were equal, or hopefully more testing, to the abilities of the guns. Alan's team, which included Gary Parsley, were pretty good shots so I presented them with difficult, high birds, which they seemed to appreciate. Alan in particular was impressed that the shoot was constantly delivering high game birds from such relatively unpromising ground. With Britain in the depths of a severe recession, both the Montagu family and Game Finders were struggling to fill all the days available, so when Alan and his team approached them both with a proposal to take the whole shoot on for their own, sole use, the offer was gratefully accepted. Therefore, for the third time in as many years, I found myself with a new employer.

I really enjoyed working directly for Alan. Again I was blessed in that I was left very much to my own devices to develop the shoot and it was clear that Alan had a very similar philosophy to me as to how he wanted the birds presented. However, the shoot perhaps became a victim of its own success in that the Montagu family, as I understand it, became somewhat concerned that the running of the Estate was becoming subordinate to the shoot. I think Alan was becoming aware that his lease might not be renewed for the 1973-74 season.

The Montagu family reassured me that an estate management role would still be there for me, but having moved into the world of commercial game shooting I was keen to continue with it. I was now more adamant than ever that I wanted to make gamekeeping my long-term career. Through a contact at Dulverton, a Dr Stuart Woodman, both Alan and I were made aware that the shooting rights on an Exmoor shoot named Miltons might be available. Dr Woodman had had the rights for Miltons but found that he frequently clashed with the landowner, a Mr Christopher Thomas-Everard, and had decided to take the shooting rights on another Exmoor shoot instead, at Molland. Dr Woodman had only shot Miltons for one season and before that no serious shooting had taken place there since 1938. Although the earliest shooting records go back to 1883, the shoot was virtually a blank canvas on which I could be left to make my own impression and this was certainly appealing to me.

Alan, too, was keen to consider the Miltons shoot, which, by the way, had no association with Alan's surname. Its location was much nearer his home in Barnstaple than Mapperton, and thus much more convenient. Alan also thought the ground would allow for some very high pheasants to be presented. He just needed a keeper to run it. He persuaded me to drive to Exmoor and view the ground. I immediately recognised that Miltons could be the next challenge that I was looking for.

CHAPTER FOUR

Miltons and the Goal of the Exmoor High Bird

The landscape of Exmoor was so different from the soft, green, rolling hills of Dorset, with which I had become so familiar. Alan Milton had made it quite clear to me that he was only prepared to take on the Miltons shoot if I agreed to become its gamekeeper, so Sally and I drove there in February 1974 for a recce. My first impression was that we were in a totally alien landscape! Indeed, I think Sally was more excited about the prospect of the move than I was. The day we chose for our visit was cold and wet. The woods were very open, the ground rocky and rugged, and I must admit that I was pretty daunted and felt somewhat ill-prepared for what I now faced. Of course, this was the challenge that I really wanted and I knew Alan and I would be able to work well together; but even so to accept the role of Head Keeper at Miltons would be something of a risk. With a young family to support, it was a proposition that had to be considered very carefully. It was not just the role that was daunting, but a move to such a remote and isolated location was not a decision to be taken lightly.

I must have changed my mind four or five times before I finally gave Alan my formal acceptance of the job he had so kindly offered me. I am certain that without his help and support, the success that Miltons has achieved, and that of many associated Exmoor shoots, would never have come to fruition. We worked so well together and had such trust in each other. I consider our relationship to have been the most perfect partnership. It was humbling that he recognised that I seem to have an inherent talent for spotting ground to produce high-bird drives and he has often complimented me on my ability to place guns correctly. Personally I have always been so grateful that Alan allowed me the freedom that he did to get on and do my job without interference. I know many gamekeepers reading these lines will have experience of a shoot owner or manager who has intervened far too often and consequently made their jobs almost impossible. I was so lucky that this was never the case with Alan. The fact that I also had the support of the other members of the syndicate – gentlemen such as David Lovall, Trevor Baker, Peter Michallat, Alfie Read, Geoffrey Ginster (of pasty fame) and Philip Chapple – made the decision to move that much easier.

It was asking a great deal of Sally to make the transition to Exmoor, especially since in our first year or so we were forced to live in a caravan. Miltons Cottage, which was to be our eventual home for five years or so, had a long-standing tenant who had to be found an alternative home and this took some time. Life in the caravan was far from comfortable and those early months were characterised by the damp and cold which seemed to percolate through the walls of the caravan whatever the weather. Sally had no access to a washing machine and all our clothes, including those for our three children, Simon, Robert and Anna, had to be hand-washed and they never seemed to dry completely.

In my first season at Miltons, working as I was solely for Alan's syndicate, we put down 3,000 or so pheasants and a few hundred duck. Today, with the sophisticated radio communications at our disposal, controlling the day is so much easier. At Mapperton and in the early days at Miltons I ran the beating line whilst Alan controlled and moved the guns. The drive would start with the firing of one shot to let me know that the guns were in position. Of course the odd mistake was made, but they were surprisingly few. Nowadays I think that the main blessing of radios is that I can stand behind the guns and watch the birds as they are presented. From this position I can readily make any adjustments to the beating line, I can move the guns if required and can even stop the drive if, for example, the wind suddenly changes direction requiring a repositioning of the guns. If, as a keeper, you are in the beating line you are not always aware of problems over in the gun-line; sometimes it is very true that you can be too close to the action to see the wider problems or consequences. Having said all that, Alan and I formed a great team and were usually able to exceed the expectations of the guns.

Having learnt from my experiences at Mapperton, I resolved to introduce myself to my new neighbours early on. Whilst I could see the potential of the ground at Miltons for producing high birds, I also saw that if we could obtain the shooting rights over nearby and adjoining land then Miltons could be transformed into something very special indeed. The number of deep valleys surrounding the shoot meant that, if we could get permission to shoot over such terrain, and plant strategically placed cover crops, then I sincerely believed that the Exmoor high pheasant would become a reality. At this early stage Alan and I had no grand strategy to produce high birds; we simply wanted to establish a good, perhaps a very good, shoot, but we could both see that if we got it right we could expect to produce some seriously high birds.

I visited a number of neighbouring farmers to try to get

them to agree to the granting of shooting rights. I wanted to do this before the presence of scores of pheasants might put them off! I stressed the opportunity to gain a reliable income from a source away from farming, on ground that was marginal for farming anyway, and also that we would need little or no input from them. We would build pheasant pens and if the farmers were required to plant a cover crop, then they would be fairly paid to do so. In addition I emphasised that the shoot would be utilising their land over the winter when it was at its least productive and we would thus keep any disruption to a minimum. I think one of my most useful assets, which I have enhanced as I have matured, learning by trial and error, is that I relate easily to people and I am able to communicate with anyone, whatever their standing or wealth. I see difficult people not as a problem but as a challenge, to be turned around to my way of thinking. Although this has taken longer with some than others, I usually get there in the end, with the help of a smile and a strong handshake.

Christopher Thomas-Everard, the landowner at Miltons, was very keen for the shoot to be a success and was certainly very supportive of me. His backing definitely helped in my negotiations with the local farmers, some of whom were his tenants. As the years went by and shooting became more of a way of life upon Exmoor, many of these local farmers, whether it was at Miltons or at the other shoots we acquired such as Bulland and Chargot, became ready helpers in the beating line, not only to earn a bit of extra cash during the quiet months, but also for the sheer fun and enjoyment of the day.

This inclusive approach also stood me in good stead when dealing with the local hunting groups. Then, even more than today, hunting was the number one pursuit on Exmoor. There were powerful opinions and strong voices in its support and my arrival at Miltons raised some interesting questions that had to be addressed. Some thought that large-scale game shooting and fox and stag hunting were not compatible. Early talk, scaremongering really, told of hounds running through pheasant drives whilst a shoot was taking place, or that ground would be lost to the hunts. However, I personally was convinced that shooting and hunting could work alongside each other, and, more importantly, for the future of the countryside they would have to do so.

My love, or rather passion, for cricket helped break down many barriers. I joined the local Bridgetown side as soon as I could and became heavily involved in both the playing and the social side of the club. Many of my team-mates were hunting men, whilst others enjoyed a bit of shooting, and I was never slow in bringing Miltons into the conversation and trying to explain what we were doing. I am sure that word soon spread and, although I still encountered some opposition, usually I could handle it with a smile and a chat. Cricket certainly helped to integrate me into Exmoor life and I made many long-lasting friendships, such as that with Doug Sherring, my captain at Bridgetown. Doug was definitely Mr Bridgetown, for he was heavily involved with the local community in general, but cricket in particular. Not only would he score, umpire and make the teas, but also cut the grass: he epitomised all that is good about village cricket. Bridgetown received the accolade of being named as *Wisden*'s Loveliest Village Cricket Ground in 2002 and so much of this success was due to Doug's hard work and commitment. Mike Hayes, who farmed on the boundary of Miltons, also became a regular cricketing companion and a great friend.

As with everything in my life, I threw myself into village cricket. Although primarily a spin bowler, I loved my batting too, and I became somewhat renowned for my hard-hitting innings as I came out at number five or six. These innings would either be very brief, as I practised my golf swing at a straight ball which took my middle stump, or I connected to make a rapid twenty or thirty before being caught in the deep. Only once did I manage to score a century, against a touring side from Balliol College, Oxford. Although I would admit that I had a few fortunate escapes on the way to my maiden century, every village cricketer, past and present, will know how satisfying such a knock is. I have lived off that innings ever since!

My bowling style was rather unorthodox, for as I released the ball I would always utter a loud grunt, just like many professional tennis players do today. I am not sure whether this noise was intentional or not, but I did manage to secure the odd wicket as the batsman either collapsed in laughter or lost his concentration! My fielding technique was legendary and has been described as 'eccentric'. I must admit I did struggle with my coordination whilst fielding and throwing. I often, in a slight panic, managed to throw the ball to the wrong end, missing chances to run out a batsman and sometimes causing overthrow runs as the bowler or wicketkeeper, or both, missed my rather erratic throw-in. On one notable occasion this resulted in a rather animated argument with one of our best and most economical bowlers, John Reed: my throw at the stumps ended up halfway down the wicket and this led to four overthrow runs being added to John's figures. He was not best pleased and our 'discussion' continued for some time, when even a beer in the pub afterwards could not calm our row down. Village cricket is serious stuff!

Our annual tours were never quite so serious though and we would often spend a very drunken and fun weekend in Cornwall playing a couple of matches between drinking sessions. We even managed one year to go on a tour to Holland, where the beer was dangerously cheap and strong, too. I learnt I had a knack of persuading people to part with their money, whether this was for a tour or just selling weekly raffle tickets for club funds. This ability has come in very useful throughout my life. I played for Bridgetown for nearly fifteen years, in two stints of ten and five years. I am delighted to maintain my connection with the cricket club and am now a Vice-President. Our annual cricket club dinner is one of the highlights of my year for it is always great to catch up with old friends and talk of the old days. I am so fortunate to have such wonderful Exmoor memories, from the playing field and also of the true, deep friendships that I was lucky enough to forge there.

Another very dear friend I made in my early days on Exmoor, who remains a very close one, is Brian Turner, operations and store manager at Butlins in Minehead. Brian's responsibilities at the holiday camp are huge and range from employing and managing the staff, to ensuring that the kitchens are able to keep all the holiday-makers fed, to the most important job of all, making sure that the beer does not run out! Brian is a local Exmoor man, with a passion for country pursuits. It was not long before our shared affinity for the countryside drew us together and Brian soon accepted the role of head picker-up at Miltons. The job fitted in well with his work at Butlins, in that he could usually escape from his duties there during the holiday camp's quiet, off-season and on occasions he would even bring along some of his staff to help out in the beating line. Brian has been a true and loyal ally, who has stuck with me throughout. He now runs the picking-up team at Castle Hill and I could not ask for a more dependable friend.

I was also blessed in that many of my Mapperton friends and colleagues came to visit me to see how I was getting on and even lent an occasional hand. Giles Wood stayed in our caravan on the occasional weekend and helped in the beating line. As I have mentioned, Keith, my old Mapperton beat-keeper, journeyed up to see me and helped load. I was also introduced to other gamekeepers in the area and would often join them in their beating lines when they were short of bodies. I went to the Rackenford shoot on numerous occasions, for the keeper, Bob Fryer, was a former colleague from my Mapperton days. I would drag my two sons, Robert and Simon, along with me to help in the line, although they were not always as keen as me. It was at Rackenford that I first met Peter Gould as I was chasing my boys around the yard after they had committed some misdemeanour. Peter would become a regular face and a wonderful friend who has stayed by my side throughout my days on Exmoor and at Castle Hill. Peter began loading at Miltons and has remained a vocal, annoying and totally dependable presence at Castle Hill. It was with the support of such good folk, and many, many more that I was able to get through those first couple of seasons at Miltons as we began to establish our reputation.

Our first winter at Miltons was particularly harsh, in that Exmoor suffered a huge deluge of snow and for weeks we were virtually cut off. Even the Army had to be called in and, using tracked vehicles and helicopters, essential food supplies were delivered by the troops. Much of my time was spent trying to keep my family warm and sheltered and helping out local farmers, such as Tom Westcott, in their searches for ewes and lambs that were buried under several feet of snow. One day Tom thanked me for my help by serving me up a meal of lamb's-tail stew, a good demonstration of the locals' way of making use of everything. Fortunately, I had greedily eaten the stew before Tom told me what was in it, for I am not sure I could have faced it if I had known what it was!

I will freely admit that my first year living on Exmoor was a difficult one. Our spartan living conditions, the pressures of establishing the shoot, and the fact that we did not really know anyone, made for some lonely times. However, helping out the likes of Tom and others, and my love of cricket, helped me to integrate. There is a saying that you are not considered a local on Exmoor until you have lived there for twenty years: I like to think that it took me considerably less time than that. What I love about Exmoor is the way that everyone does get to know one another and you do feel part of a larger community. On the other hand, the downside is that if you make a mistake, either professionally or personally, it will become general knowledge! However, an awareness of this has made me think twice on occasions and that has certainly not been a bad thing.

Despite our poor living conditions, I think our young family enjoyed living on Exmoor. The children went to the village school at Winsford and I was always keen to kick them out of the damp caravan to enjoy and experience our beautiful, if sometimes rather harsh, countryside. Rob in particular spent many hours fishing for trout and grayling in the River Exe, which was in close proximity to our home. Rob was adept at placing out nightlines over the nearby bridge to catch eels. Much to his credit, he was not only very good at catching his prey, but he soon developed a business brain as he sold the eels to his school teachers the following day. My work, and perhaps my dedication to it, meant that family outings and holidays were a rare thing and I suppose much of my contact with the children was based around me placing them in the beating line!

Looking back, my involvement of our children in the shoot might now be considered a form of child abuse. I don't know whether they had any choice in the matter but they were part of the beating team from a very young age. My boys, when aged around six or seven, were detailed with the task of stationing themselves at a place called Rock Head, which bordered the shooting ground of Miltons and land worked by Christopher Thomas-Everard. I devised a plan whereby flags were put out at night before a shoot day, so as to deter the pheasants from straying off the shoot's ground at this vulnerable 'leakage-point'. First thing of a shoot day morning, whilst it was still dark, I would load the lads into the back of the Subaru pick-up and leave them up at Rock Head. I left them with clear instructions to walk up and down the length of the placed flags, tapping them to make both noise and movement, in the hope of pushing the pheasants back. On some days the boys would be left to their lonely task from very early morning dark until lunchtime, in all weathers. As you can probably tell, the success of the shoot came first! As the boys got older, they joined the beating line and I think the daily pay of five pounds was a good enough incentive to draw them out, again in all weathers. Later they got involved more directly in the shoot when Sally cooked and served-up her much appreciated shoot lunches. During the season, the cottage would have a stream of folk – whether beaters, pickers-up or guns – coming and going all the time and there was always a great social atmosphere. Of the three children, Rob in particular seemed to enjoy the outdoor life and as he grew up it took little persuasion for him to go out and help under-keepers and beat-keepers with feeding and other daily tasks.

I still recall very fondly my early rough shooting experiences and the joy and fun such days gave me. I was keen that when time allowed I would set aside time not only for my own enjoyment but also for others. Rough shooting is a fabulous way to bond with folk, make friendships and introduce youngsters to the world of shooting. The problem was that I was so busy that making and finding time proved rather difficult. I resolved that I would introduce something of a tradition and set aside each Christmas Eve whilst I was at Miltons to take a gang of friends and colleagues out on a full rough shooting day, whatever the weather. To be frank, the pressure on my colleagues and me was such that this day was a great opportunity for us to unwind and let off some steam. I would arrange for my merry band of men, and dogs, to be dropped off at a site above Withypool, which was roughly a ten-mile walk, as the crow flies, back to Miltons. Miltons had the shooting rights to this ground, but it is predominantly top moor land that we did not utilise, although it was used for hunting. With no other large pheasant shoots in the area at this time our 'bag' was often meagre and usually consisted of the odd snipe and maybe a woodcock or two. The day had few rules but the central one was that each of us carried a bottle of either whisky or port and if by chance we did manage to claim a bird for the bag, we would stop, form a circle and down one of the bottles between us. Fortunately, for the sake of both our livers and our shooting safety, the total bag was always a low one. Although never drunk, by the time we descended upon our house at Miltons in the dark early evening of Christmas Eve we were quite merry. My then wife Sally would produce a wonderful roast meal and our laughter, and drinking, would continue. Memorable times.

I have never been one to stay still for long, whether in my day's work or in terms of longer-term planning. As a gamekeeper I feel I must always be looking afresh at ground, seeing how drives can be improved or adapted and considering new possibilities. In those first years I was fortunate enough to visit the Gurston Down shoot in Wiltshire, situated between Salisbury and Shaftesbury, where, under the inspired leadership of David Hitchings, it had gained recognition as *the* high bird shoot in the south-west. I observed for a couple of days and was able to grasp exactly what David and his team had achieved over the chalk valleys. I witnessed many wonderful high birds and naturally my mind moved back to the terrain at Miltons where I knew that, with some hard work and application, something very special could also be achieved. Of course the topography at Miltons would supply me with a great opportunity, for with driven drives at over 1,000 feet above sea level at their highest point, the potential for some seriously high birds was there.

In my second season at Miltons, I distinctly remember Alan approaching me after one of the more speculative drives and saying that we would have to move the guns further up the slopes as by the time the birds passed over the valley floor, they were too testing and too high for the guns. These words were music to my ears! Alan had been in the England Clay Pigeon Down-the-Line team since 1961 and was Captain in 1977. He was a marvellous shot. If the birds were proving too demanding for people like him and the syndicate guns, then clearly the future of Miltons as a champion of the Exmoor high pheasant was looking promising.

Despite my delight in Alan's words, I also took on board what he was really saying. In stating that he thought the birds were too high for the abilities of some of the syndicate guns, he was simultaneously making the point that there is no fun in missing: it does not take long for a gun to become disillusioned, with the result that he or she does not enjoy their day. Ever since, I have viewed my job as one of customer service. Yes, I have taken great pride and delight in showing high birds, and there is now a ready market for top quality guns to shoot top quality birds. However, by definition, not everyone is in this league and even today at Castle Hill we can adjust the day to some extent so that the birds are within the abilities of most guns. The last thing I want is for a team of guns to leave a shoot disheartened. I aim that all go away having had a cracking day and having shot some memorable birds.

The world of shooting is a very small, sometimes incestuous one. This certainly means that word can spread very quickly if you are doing something good – or bad! It did not take long for what Alan and I were trying to achieve at Miltons to come to the attention of the shooting Press and suddenly we were being written and spoken of as either pioneers or heretics, depending upon the different points of view. The Press were keen to visit our little part of Exmoor and I recall one particular occasion when Gordon Carlisle of the *Shooting Times* descended on us to attend a shoot day in November 1979. His article, of which I still have a copy, appeared in print in December of that year and reading it today brings back some wonderful memories. The guns on this particular day included Graham Thorner, Geoffrey Ginster, Jeffrey Saunders and Philip Chapple, with Alan as a walking gun. It is worth quoting directly from Gordon Carlisle's article. I think he really captured the then unique qualities of a shoot day at Miltons:

> *'As the Guns wait along the combe bottom there is no sound except the splashing of the stream, tumbling towards the main valley and the river Exe. Suddenly three pheasants come sailing out over the crest 100 feet above, flying fast and then gliding, making for the mixed woodland just behind the line. Three or four shots, two birds fly on and one drops, taking countable seconds to reach the ground... As a drive develops it is quite uncanny to watch some of these*

high pheasants appear so quietly and almost unexpectedly. Only later do the approaching beaters become audible, forcing their way through dense undergrowth, so far untouched by frost, and pushing on down the precipitous slopes. In some places the ground is so sheer and dotted with large rocks that even dogs can scarcely climb up it. The pickers-up have a tough job which the shoot acknowledges by having plenty of them, nine on the day of my visit.'

The article continued:

'Mr Milton encourages initiative and efficiency, as two examples illustrate. The beaters' trailer is an unusual vehicle, which gives cover from rain; once used by the Electricity Board for cables and repair equipment, it now has seats instead of shelves and lockers. All shoots must sell their game for the best price obtainable, to offset ever-increasing costs; plucked and dressed birds realise more than fully feathered ones, and so the keeper operates a plucking machine, and his wife nobly cleans the birds, which are then sold to local hotels and restaurants.'

Concluding the article, Gordon Carlisle recorded that:

'The main syndicate rose to the occasion on this challenging day… and the bag was 409 pheasants. The number of shots? 1,480, a ration of 1 to 3.6 and that was very good shooting.'

Indeed it was, and coverage like this meant that shooting folk began to realise that something special was happening at Miltons.

During the time that the shoot was run on behalf of the syndicate, money was always tight. In the beginning we had all roughed it with a basic lunch in a draughty barn or out in the open, but with higher expectations for comfort we eventually ended each day with a large meal cooked by my wife back at Miltons Cottage. This was just one factor which placed increasing financial demands upon the guns. Others included an ever-increasing number of birds put down, expansion on to neighbouring ground, larger pens, and the hire of a beat-keeper, named Derek Watts. Alan Milton met my requests for more funds with a smile and what I asked for I usually got, but I could see that if Miltons was to continue to expand we would have to consider going down the commercial route and letting out some days. I sincerely felt that with coverage such as the *Shooting Times* article, guns would be willing to travel to Exmoor to experience what we could offer and pay good money to do so. I approached Alan with this idea and I think we were both rather fearful of where this might lead; but after six years and with some syndicate guns dropping away, we had little alternative. However, we were very much aware that we would be breaking a long-standing taboo on Exmoor, in that shooting should be by invitation only and not for commercial gain. We were stepping on to dangerous ground.

Through a contact Alan knew at the Littlecott Estate near Hungerford, where the syndicate had bought a couple of days a season for a number of years, we learnt of Roxtons sporting agency, run by a gentleman named Chris Orssich. Alan did some research and received back favourable reports concerning the agency. Once the decision had been made for us to consider letting some days at Miltons, it seemed only right to find out if Roxtons would be interested. Chris duly travelled down to Exmoor during the off-season and Alan and I gave him a guided tour. He clearly liked what he saw of the ground and also must have seen the shoot's potential for producing the testing, high birds that many of his clients demanded. Initially the company took two days for the following season.

Although I had confidence in the shoot – the ground we were working over and the team that I had around me – I was still terribly nervous when the day came for our first commercial booking. That was in November 1981, when a gentleman named Alan Mann, who came from Cobham in Surrey, arrived with a team of eight guns for a 250-bird day. My nerves and my concerns for the day disappeared as soon as the first few pheasants appeared on the initial drive. The birds were all that I hoped they would be: high, very high in fact, and curling. All of Alan Mann's team, as well as Chris Orssich, were pretty impressed, to put it mildly. After what he had witnessed, Chris knew that Roxtons would have little difficulty in marketing and selling days at Miltons. He later said to me that he thought he had seen high birds until he realised what Miltons could offer. From the following season onwards, the agency was keen to book as many days as possible and to this day Roxtons remains the sole agent for Miltons. Alan Milton was still keen to have a few days for himself, and some of his great friends, such as Tom Greenham, bought odd days, but otherwise Roxtons snapped up any that were available.

Within the space of one season, with the support of Roxtons, the shoot had gone from being a once-a-week syndicate shoot, with a couple of let days, to one that provided three or four commercially sold days every week. Needless to say, my life was transformed! Not only did the number of birds have to increase dramatically but the pressures on shoot days were significantly raised because now we were attracting some of the top guns in the world to our tiny part of Exmoor. Some of these individuals had seen the best and expected the best and, although many were demanding customers, Alan Milton and I prided ourselves that both we and the Miltons shoot consistently exceeded their high expectations. Many of these guns were delightful people who became, and remain, good friends.

The usual format for the day would be four drives in the morning, followed by one of Sally's legendary lunches. We would then manage another two drives in the afternoon. The terrain of deep valleys was, of course, ideal to show high birds. The careful use of cover crops and trees could enhance the birds' height even more. Alan and I never felt that we had to conceal the guns in the line in any way, for few birds broke out of the sides of the drives or went back. Although the birds were obliging in that sense, once their wings were locked into a glide it was soon apparent that many guns could be deceived by their speed. If there was even a breath of wind on a shoot day, then the ability to calculate accurately the speed of the bird became even more of a challenge. I can honestly say that few birds were missed by guns in front at Miltons, but nearly always behind! In addition, I saw many guns miss what they perceived to be relatively easy straight ones coming towards them, for they had not recognised that their target was sliding or curling on the wind and thus shot down the side of the bird.

Sir Edward Goschen, who is a lovely man, a true gentleman, and has contributed so much to the development of shooting on Exmoor, had a rather poor day when he first shot at Miltons. Indeed, I think he was rather humbled by the experience, but he returned again and again and soon learnt how to 'tame' the 'Miltons bird'! Our guns wanted the best, expected the best and were prepared to pay for the best. At that time there were few shoots on which guns could expect to shoot 150 cartridges on a peg at seriously challenging birds, but we were able to supply both the quantity and the quality of shooting that many folk were searching for. The birds we were able to present were pretty special and testing enough for even the most experienced gun; and this, of course, is the basis of the shoot's success and reputation.

Through Roxtons' worldwide connections we had many foreign visitors. One syndicate that was always well received was the self-styled 'New York Big Shots', led by shoot captain Jack Lapsley. The team, including such individuals as Nelson Doubleday Jr and David Kirkland, would fly into Heathrow and then journey to the south-west for a week at a time. Two days would be spent at Miltons, with a couple of other days shooting elsewhere, all arranged by Roxtons.

My first wife, Sally, was responsible at that time for feeding all the teams that came to Miltons, and we somehow managed to squeeze fifteen or so folk into our small dining-room for lunch on each shoot day. Here Sally would serve her renowned traditional roasts, followed by delights such as apple crumble. I recall that the Americans in particular loved this British fare. Roxtons' Chris Orssich delighted in teasing Sally, or as she would call it tormenting, on shoot days and would always be thinking of the next practical joke he could play on her or her helper, Jackie. One particular memory that stays with me was when Chris stretched cling-film over the toilet bowl. When Jackie answered a call of nature she was rather traumatised by the results! On another occasion, Chris managed to attach two stink bombs under the same loo seat and this time Sally was the butt of the joke. She did, I recall, get her own back, in that she managed to gain access to Chris's room at the Royal Oak at Winsford and sewed up a pair of his long johns, which caused him great confusion the following morning…

After each day, those guns that were staying over were accommodated at the Royal Oak in Winsford. I managed to persuade the then landlord, Charles Stevens, that it would be a great idea to open his doors to shooting parties. I think he might have regretted that decision in the early days, when several of the nights took on the characteristics of an over-enthusiastic rugby tour. On occasions, I would have to stay overnight too. This was especially the case if Peter Gould was present, for he is such a bad influence on me. I do remember that Peter would always ask that any drinks that he or I consumed were put on Room 13's tab: I would like to take this opportunity to apologise to any of the guns who stayed at the Royal Oak at that time and were surprised by some rather hefty room bills. Sorry!

On one memorable evening someone, and I really can't remember who, thought it would be a good idea to smuggle a pair of geese into David Kirkland's bedroom. When David returned to his room, after several beers, he was confronted by two very angry geese and a mountain of goose poo all over his bed! David did gain some revenge on a later occasion, when he got hold of a donkey that belonged to the landlord and shut it in Chris Orssich's room. Chris discovered his room in a similar state to David's, only on a grander scale. After this, the landlord put paid to such high jinx, which was probably for the best.

I suppose many guns did view me as something of an oddball in the world of gamekeeping for, unlike those of the 'old school', I was very much prepared to join a team of guns for a drink at the end of the day, and shout and holler with the best of them, as well as take the mickey out of them during the shoot day. For the vast majority of guns, though, my approach was welcome and many became good friends.

The New York Big Shots became regulars and firm favourites with us all at Miltons. These gentlemen could both give and take a joke, which always eased some of the pressure on me. On one particular day I arranged that we would shoot a drive near the Bridgetown Cricket Club called 'Bridgetown Wood'. Just at the moment that the first birds appeared, a van with four loudspeakers drove past playing the American national anthem, 'The Star-Spangled Banner'. I had hoped and expected that the Big Shots team would respect their national anthem and stop shooting or, at the very least, be put off. Neither of these things happened, for they carried on shooting as well as ever and even continued to do so when the van returned, playing the tunes 'The Ballad of Davy Crockett' and 'The Yellow Rose of Texas'. Although my plan had failed, we were able to have a good laugh about it later in the Royal Oak. On another occasion I arranged for some clay traps to be located on a bank in the middle of one of our partridge drives. As the birds flew towards the line, they were joined by several clays. The Americans were unfazed even by this, and remained completely single-minded in their shooting of the partridge.

Over the years, the Big Shots became firm friends. Jack and Hopey Lapsley invited Sally and me over to the States one spring.

Whilst we were there, Nelson Doubleday Jr also took it upon himself to entertain us. He owned the New York Mets baseball team and we were guests at one of the matches, along with President Bush's wife, Barbara, and Mayor Koch of New York. This all felt a million miles away from Exmoor, let alone my early days at Sherborne. We were looked after like royalty and stayed on Long Island, at Jack and Hopey Lapsley's house, travelling daily into Manhattan to see the sights. It was such a memorable visit and I count myself so privileged not only to have been invited to make such a trip but also to have made such wonderful friends through the sport of shooting.

Our relationship with Roxtons flourished and it seemed to take no time at all for our reputation for providing high birds to become established. We never had to advertise days and, although we did get coverage in the shooting Press, it was Roxtons' contacts all over the world that filled our let days. Everything seemed to happen so quickly. Suddenly, Miltons was on the list of 'must' shoots and we were struggling to keep up with the demand. The Dukes of Westminster and Roxburghe became regular clients, as did Patrick Lichfield, Captain Mark Phillips and HRH Prince Michael of Kent. European royalty, including HRH Prince Bernhard of the Netherlands and the then Prince of Lichtenstein, were frequent guests. Sporting stars were also visitors; cricketer Ian Botham and show-jumper David Broome were seen in the shooting line as well as many other famous folk whom I had better not name. In addition, many of the top high-bird shots, gentlemen such as Tony Ball, Phil Fussell, and Bill Joyce, often shot at Miltons.

With the growth of the shoot, Sally and I moved to Holland Farm, along with our ever-increasing family now including Lisa. The extra space allowed us to construct a proper shoot room in which Sally, with the help of Janet Hawkins, served up wonderful traditional meals three or four times a week for our eager and hungry guns. Today, many local folk are keen to help out on Exmoor shoots, whether as beaters or pickers-up, but in our early days we were forced to send vehicles to Minehead to collect our helpers. The idea of large-scale shooting on Exmoor was still alien to many back then, as hunting was still of such paramount importance.

Looking back, I am surprised that in fact shooting and hunting were so readily able to accommodate each other's demands, and I can only think of one explosive moment during my time on Exmoor. Late one afternoon, just as the light was fading and the birds were going to roost and thus should not have been disturbed, the local hunt rode right over our shooting ground. I must admit that I had a bit of a set-to over this with one of the huntsmen, a certain Robert Clapworthy. Although we played cricket together and enjoyed each other's company, this incident cast a shadow over our relationship for some years. However, this was very much an isolated incident.

Although I was always grateful if the hunt could arrange to have their day's sport when we weren't shooting, this was not always possible. I did make it clear to all that if the hunt was in pursuit of a stag or a fox and the quarry was clearly running towards our shooting ground, then the hunt had priority, and we never had any major conflicts over this. Indeed, I have always tried to be supportive of hunting. Over the years I have organised and run several charity clay-pigeon days for the benefit of hunt funds. Then in 2002, for the Countryside March in London that in the end attracted the support of more than 400,000 country folk, in opposition to the proposed hunting ban, I personally organised eight coaches to take protesters from Devon and Somerset to London. There are several memories of that day that stay with me, but two things I am particularly proud of are that, despite the huge numbers involved, there was no trouble and when the march was over the streets were completely clear of rubbish. This just goes to show what respect country folk have for their country, both rural and urban.

The new-found fame of the Miltons shoot was once displayed in a rather comical way. Paul Hogan, the Australian actor featured in the *Crocodile Dundee* films, was for several years also the face of the Foster's lager television advertisements. The premise of one campaign was that this very Australian actor would be seen in very English surroundings, such as at the Royal Ballet or at a show jumping event, where he would be shown drinking Foster's, the 'amber nectar'. Paul would have a funny line at the end of the advert that cleverly highlighted his ignorance of what he was witnessing, whilst at the same time slightly taking the mickey out of the British. The adverts were a great success. Completely out of the blue, via Christopher Thomas-Everard, I received a phone call from the advertising agency asking whether Miltons could set up a simulated driven shoot, in which Paul Hogan would be watching the proceedings and would then deliver one of his characteristic punchlines. As filming was to take place during the summer, and would thus not interrupt the shooting season, I was happy to oblige.

Having agreed to the filming, I soon regretted my decision, for I quickly realised how much work it would involve. The film company asked me to arrange for some pretty local girls to be in the film and I also had to make sure that some likely guns, dressed in the finest tweeds, were standing in the shooting line. I was able to obtain both requirements from amongst my regular team of loaders, pickers-up and beaters, although some of them looked rather out of place in tweeds! Of course, I was also expected to produce some birds to fly over the 'guns', which proved to be pretty difficult for at that time of the year the only birds on the shoot were ex-lay hens, which had been 'brailled' with wing tapes so that they could not fly out of their open-top pens.

There was great excitement on the day of filming, not so much at the presence of a major Hollywood star, but at the sight of the enormous, elaborate catering caravan that slowly edged its way along the lanes of Exmoor to keep the crew and cast fed and watered throughout the day. For me, that first cup of coffee was the highlight of the day, as the filming went from bad to worse.

First of all, having removed the wing tapes from a number of birds, I just could not get them even to take off, let alone fly towards the so-called guns. I was in the pen, diving in stinging nettles, screaming and shouting to get the birds to fly; despite my best efforts, this simply wasn't going to happen. In the end we had to get a couple of dogs into the pen to 'encourage' the birds in their acting career and although the birds had little height on them they did at least fly in the right direction. All our efforts were initially wasted when the 'guns' pretended to shoot at the hapless birds, for we had loaded the 12 bores with blank cartridges and these produced copious amounts of smoke that hung in the valley. The result was that the gun line was completely obscured and filming had to stop whilst we waited for a breeze to remove the offending smokescreen. In the meantime there was nothing we could do but seek refuge in the catering caravan. If it wasn't for all the effort that had been, and was, being put into the filming that day, this small disaster might have been very comical. Looking back, it was, but just not at the time!

Despite the early setbacks I still had my big moment to come, for the director had decided that I should be given a line to speak in the closing scene with Paul Hogan. Why the director thought that my inclusion in the advert would be a good idea was a mystery, for although I think I possess some talents, acting is certainly not one of them. I could not remember the line on the day so I certainly cannot recall it now, but my scene involved me sitting at a table opposite Paul whilst he delivered a line, then I had to respond, and finally he would deliver his customary quip. Not only did I repeatedly get my line wrong, I was also constantly late with my delivery. The more errors I made, the worse I became, as nerves got the better of me. Paul tried to make things easier for me and he was very gracious, although I could sense that the director was losing his patience! To help me with my timing, Paul said that when it was my turn to speak he would kick me under the table. The problem was that the first time he did this Paul kicked me so hard on the shin that I shouted out in pain and another 'take' was ruined. Finally, after what seemed like hours, the director announced that with the earlier problems with the shooting scene and my very many errors the crew were down to the last of their film and that we only had enough left for one more 'take'. This news, rather than terrify me even more, seemed to concentrate my thoughts and I was finally able to deliver the line correctly. This was met with much relief all round and by cheers from the crew!

The film crew returned to London and the advert was edited. It was decided to trial the advert in the so-called Central television area of the Midlands, centred on Birmingham, so as to gauge audience reaction before it was shown nationally. I understand the trial lasted only two nights before an outcry from folk opposed to shooting caused the Foster's company to pull this particular advert, which was something of a shame. I never did get to see how brilliant I was at acting. Needless to say, this was my one and only appearance!

I suppose I was fortunate in so many ways at Miltons. To have the support of Alan Milton was so helpful, as was having a reliable team around me, but being in control of ground that had not really been shot over before was crucial for it allowed me to introduce drives and introduce innovations. Cover crops had not been much used before, and although the elevation of the ground meant that we could not grow maize, we made much use of kale. I was able to thin out the woodlands and plant rhododendrons so as to warm up the woods and make them more attractive to the birds, which of course helped to stop them wandering.

Alan and I, having seen the success of French red-legged partridge at Gurston Down, were convinced we could make them work at Miltons. The introduction of partridge to Exmoor was seen then as a radical move and perhaps by some as even a step too far, but with the terrain we had I felt sure we would soon gain a favourable reputation. The biggest problem we faced was that the normal cover crops that partridge love, such as maize, simply could not be grown on Exmoor, due to its altitude and unpredictable weather. Instead we tried kale, mustard, buckwheat and gorse, and the latter worked surprisingly well. Starting in early September, we began to provide back-to-back partridge days, before moving on to pheasant at the end of October. This, of course, extended the shooting season by at least a month and enhanced the revenue for the shoot. Drives such as Ariel, Church and Triangle became renowned high partridge drives and helped to further enhance Miltons' reputation. Within the space of one season we were offering driven partridge days of between 250 and 500 birds, which seems astonishing now. Our client base, many of whom were used to having to travel to Spain or further afield for driven partridge, were delighted that we were able to provide such numbers and over such wonderful topography.

Our first venture into partridge was in 1981 when we put down 1,400 red-legs and seventy greys as something of a trial. Whilst the red-legs flourished and produced some memorable days, the greys simply could not cope with the Exmoor climate. Following the success with the red-legs, their numbers were increased to 3,000 in 1982, which allowed us to sell seven 300-bird partridge days that year, alongside twenty-five 300-bird pheasant days and four duck days. We limited our driven partridge days to one long, deep valley and throughout the day of usually five or six drives the guns were moved along the length of the valley. This provided them with some stunningly high partridge. The birds were basically driven from game crop to game crop across the guns from hill peak to hill peak. This may sound all very simple but for such a plan to work successfully we had to be clever with both the siting of the game crops and the type used but, most importantly, we had to be very organised and disciplined in our beating so as to get the birds to fly over the guns as well as not flush all at once. Anyone who has beaten or shot partridge will know how difficult and unpredictable the birds can be.

The sporting Press showed as much interest in our partridge days as it had done in our pheasant. For example, in mid-September 1982, we were visited on our third driven partridge day of that season by David Goodchild of *Sporting Gun*, who wrote an article that later appeared in the November 1982 issue. David was suitably impressed by the height of the birds and we were fortunate in that we had a cracking team of guns shooting that day, including Bill Joyce and Martin Reynolds, who did full justice to the birds. David particularly enjoyed the Triangle drive and his article quoted Bill Joyce who said, 'I've been to a lot of places and they [the birds] don't come higher.'

We reached our 300-bird bag after five drives, three in the morning and two after lunch. I recall that the day was particularly sunny in the morning and, being a perfectionist and a worrier, I was not happy with how the birds had flown on the first two drives. Fortunately, however, some cloud did finally appear and the last three drives satisfied even me!

Of course, with no drives really in existence before Alan Milton took on the shoot, it was up to us to think of names. Many of the woodland drives were easy to name, such as Howe Wood, a favourite with many guns for the constant stream of high birds it produces. Some drives were christened after local characters, such as Tom's Hedges, or natural features such as The Rookery or Miltons' Rocks. However, my favourite was named by my good friend from Mapperton, George Brown, who travelled to Miltons to load for us on occasions. Standing next to George one day as the birds came over the gun line, he turned to me and said, 'Brian, those birds are out of reach!' Straightaway I thought this would be a great name to sum-up Miltons and Out-of-Reach became a well-known and much requested drive.

However, I would like to stress that it has never been my aim, whether at Miltons, Castle Hill or anywhere else, to send a large number of birds over the gun line that are out of range. Yes, on some drives there will be birds that are excessively high, but I am targeting for the vast majority of the birds to be between sixty and eighty yards up. In other words, high, but still well within killing distance. The challenge I set myself is to ensure that these birds are challenging in other ways: curling, sliding, dipping, anything to make them difficult for the guns. I have found that over the years the guns who shoot at places like Miltons or Castle Hill want to be seriously challenged, but also want to know that they have killed their targets.

Despite my best efforts to expand Miltons on to neighbouring land, we reached our then practical maximum at around 3,000 acres (although it has since expanded to over 5,000 acres) and by the early eighties we were shooting four times a week, although we could have filled seven days a week! The demand to shoot Exmoor high birds was such that it became clear to Alan Milton and me that if we could find suitable ground nearby we could establish other shoots similar in size and scope to Miltons. Roxtons, as aware as we were of the potential demand, encouraged Alan and me in our search. It was not long before I found myself in the role of Shoot Head Keeper, supervising the additional shoots of Chargot, on the edge of Exmoor overlooking the Bristol Channel, and Bulland, near Wiveliscombe in Somerset.

The ground at Bulland had never been shot over before, but on my travels around the area I saw the potential for the ground to produce high birds. So, in 1982, I approached the landowner and, to my delight, my proposal to establish a shoot was readily welcomed. My direct, simple approach of knocking on front doors paid off and soon some of the land of the adjoining farms was brought into the shoot too. I appointed a Head Keeper, Mark Atkinson, who looked after the pheasants and the shoot days, whilst my role was to focus on devising drives, the placement of cover crops and direct contact with Roxtons.

Mark had worked for me for one year at Miltons as a beat-keeper and in that short space of time had clearly demonstrated his love of the job as well as his ability. I had no reservations whatsoever in appointing him as Keeper at Bulland. As the ground had never been shot over before, Mark's job involved a great deal of early public relations with the locals and he also had to bring his own team of beaters, loaders and pickers-up on-board, whom he was able to reward with a really superb 'beaters' day' shoot at the end of each season. Although I gave him some support, the success of the shoot in those first few years rests largely with Mark. On shoot days he was helped by either Alan Milton or Richard Jenkins who 'hosted' the days, thus relieving him of some of the pressure.

Bulland is blessed with some wonderful high bird drives, including Bulland Ford. When we were looking for inspiration to name some of the other drives, the discovery of an abandoned Hillman Imp car in one of the woods led us to call this particular drive 'Imp'. Mark worked with an under-keeper, John Brooks, who later helped me establish Challacombe, between Simonsbath and Blackmoor Gate, as a high partridge shoot.

Another likely piece of shooting ground, which I had had my eye on for some time, was at Chargot. Negotiations here were complicated by the fact that the land was split between a father and son, Sir Edward Malet and his son Harry, who did not see eye-to-eye on most things. Alan Milton had already been in conversation with Harry Malet about the possibility of acquiring the shooting rights and I sincerely believe that Alan's reputation for fairness and integrity was the key to securing a deal with Harry on the death of his father. Once I knew that Alan had been successful, I again approached adjoining farmers and was able to secure sufficient ground to establish the Chargot shoot, with Nick Boniface as my Head Keeper, and my son Robert as a beat-keeper. Robert, following his days helping out at Miltons, had fallen into the life of game-keeping and he worked at Chargot and West Molland before setting up and establishing the North Molton shoot. I remember that I was overseeing a day at Chargot when Robert supervised his very first drive, which happened to be one of the shoot's signature drives. After it had been shot I took great delight in telling Robert how proud I was of him, a pride that remains with me, as he has done so well in developing North Molton into a classic and great shoot.

Chargot has now become synonymous with the best pheasant and partridge shooting that the West Country has to offer. As soon as I saw the ground, with valley upon valley of perfect shooting topography, I knew we could present some incredibly high birds. This soon proved to be the case and, under the keepership of Nick, Chargot has gone from strength to strength. Drives such as Trebra, renamed 'Spitfire' by the former owner, Charles Church (who owned but also sadly died in a Spitfire crash), Chimney and Melanie's have a fully justified, worldwide reputation for astonishing birds and I am very proud to have played a part in the establishment of the shoot. I can remember Tony Ball shooting on Trebra on one occasion when, using his favourite cartridge, a Rottweil Tiger, he shot a partridge that was so high he was able to lower his gun and reload before the dead bird hit the ground!

Chargot is now shot over 4,500 acres and the topography is such that cover crops are the key to the shoot's success. The norm is for strips of kale, spring barley and maize to be alternated in long rows, up to nine metres wide, across the length of fields. Indeed, in excess of 400 acres are planted in cover crops. I believe Chargot's success is firmly based on good customer service. I know Nick Boniface always makes the guns feel very welcome. Also, especially in November, Chargot does offer some wonderful combined high partridge and pheasant shooting to delight those fortunate enough to be able to shoot there.

As Shoot Head Keeper for Miltons, Bulland and Chargot I felt that sometimes I didn't have a moment to breathe. Even I have learnt over the years that you can't be in two places at once, despite your best efforts. On shoot days I would host at one of the shoots, whilst Alan Milton and Richard Jenkins would be at the other two. A representative from Roxtons – Chris, Mark Firth or later Dan Reynolds – would also be at each to offer their support.

When we weren't actually shooting I would find myself dashing between the three shoots and this is when my love of fast driving was a benefit. Trying to save time one day at Bulland, I decided to take my Subaru through a ford in a stream that was swollen by heavy rain. My companions yelled at me not to attempt the crossing, but I ploughed on regardless, only to come to a complete stop halfway across, with an engine that took an instant dislike to its surroundings and decided to die in a rather loud and spectacular fashion! We had to wade to dry land and the vehicle was yet another write-off for Alan Milton to deal with. Apparently my sometimes erratic and wayward driving caused me to have something of a reputation; I have even heard folk say that they would not buy a second-hand vehicle from me in the afternoon, if I had driven it out of the showroom brand-new in the morning!

At one stage we were employing nineteen full-time staff, as well as a small army of beaters and pickers-up, using eighteen vehicles and working six days a week, on the three shoots. Such a mad, hectic lifestyle finally took its toll. After one particularly stupid week, I was soaking in a lovely, warm bath but when I tried to get out, I found that my body had virtually seized up or locked with exhaustion. My wife somehow managed to pull me out of the cooling water before I died of hypothermia, but this episode really shocked me and made me slow down a little, for a while at least.

Although I was frantically busy, it was what I enjoyed and I was extremely happy with my life. Yet, out of nowhere, I was hit one day with the realisation that I might be forced to move from my beloved Miltons. Although I would admit that my role of Shoot Head Keeper was indeed a challenging one, both mentally and physically, I was, as I say, extremely happy in what I was doing and I loved the Exmoor life. However, in the January of 1987 I received a phone call from Alan Milton to come along to his offices in Barnstaple for a chat. Alan, to his immense credit, and with great dignity, informed me that he had to deliver the sad news that he had decided to sell on the shooting rights of the three shoots of Miltons, Bulland and Chargot. I was completely dumbfounded and for once almost speechless. I was finally able to gather my thoughts enough to enquire what was happening.

Alan explained that the property developer, Charles Church, had approached him with an offer to buy the rights to all three shoots. Charles had settled on a price with the landowners concerned and had agreed a level of compensation with Alan. My first thought was for the welfare of the keeping staff but Alan was able to reassure me that they would all be retained. However he also told me that the new owner did not want me to continue in my role as Shoot Head Keeper, supervising all three shoots, but was prepared for me to accept the position as Head Keeper at Miltons. Charles had also lined up Steve Potter, from a company called Southern Partridges, to supervise the day-to-day running of the shoots. In retrospect I think Steve and Charles knew full well that I viewed all three shoots as my babies and that I would not want to let go of the passion I had for them. Alan had given me such freedom in my role as Shoot Head Keeper and I know I would have found it extremely difficult to relinquish that freedom.

Despite the fact that Charles and Steve had a plan that did not include me in my existing position, I decided, after some thought, to go back to Alan and say that that was all I was really interested in doing. This of course put me at odds with Charles and Steve. During what was beginning to turn into a series of rather awkward conversations, I received a phone call from a gentleman named Michael Rivkin, a syndicate member at the Castle Hill shoot just outside Barnstaple. Michael informed me that Alan Milton had been contacted for his views on my abilities as a Head Keeper. Apparently Alan had been lavish in his praise and had said that he thought there would be no one better in the position. Michael told me that the syndicate leader, Commander Sam MacDonald-Hall RN, wished to meet me in the Castle Hotel in Taunton in just two days' time.

Although Castle Hill was solely a syndicate shoot at this

time, it was a very substantial one, where around 25,000 birds were put down each season: so I knew that a role there would be a significant challenge. Michael Rivkin offered no immediate explanation as to the reason for the meeting, although I could, of course, hazard a guess. Ever since Alan had told me of the change of ownership at Miltons and the other shoots, my life had been in turmoil and I was wracked with worry. I had by now left my first wife, Sally, and I was living with my present wife, Angie. We had just moved into a lovely house on the Miltons estate. Angie, who was a local Dulverton girl, had many friends in the area and we were both very keen to remain on Exmoor. I was not yet forty years of age and had still young children to support, so these few days were incredibly upsetting for both Angie and me. However, I felt that I had nothing to lose by attending the Friday meeting.

I was due to be supervising at Bulland on that Friday, but managed to excuse myself early to go down to Taunton to meet Commander MacDonald-Hall. He was very direct in his approach and almost before my bottom had had a chance to warm the seat I was offered the position of Head Keeper at Castle Hill. Naturally I was aware of the shoot and had in fact, on occasions, turned up to load there when the keeper was short-staffed.

Although the incumbent Castle Hill Head Keeper, David Moore, was a very reliable and competent man, I think that some of the syndicate members wanted Castle Hill to develop its potential more fully and did not believe that David was the person to do this. The Commander's son, Caspar MacDonald-Hall, and some of the younger syndicate members such as Michael and John Chandris had shot several times at Miltons and had clearly been impressed by what had been achieved there. I think it was due to their initiative that the Commander approached me, and, as I say, duly offered me the position of Head Keeper at Castle Hill. I was flattered to be asked, for not only did the shoot have a good reputation already but I knew it also had great potential and, if I was allowed to, I felt sure I could stamp my own style and thoughts upon the shoot and really move it forward. It was a challenge that I felt I could relish. However, there was some awkwardness in that I was friends with David Moore, and I certainly did not want to be the reason for his departure. Commander MacDonald-Hall assured me that David was leaving anyway and would receive a good settlement, so bearing this in mind I gave the offer careful consideration.

I suppose I was somewhat naïve in thinking that I would be given time, at least the weekend, to consider the offer I had just received; but the Commander informed me that I had until six p.m. to make up my mind, or the offer would be withdrawn. To be honest, I had little to decide upon. Although Angie and I would be very sad to leave Miltons and Exmoor, I had the sense to realise that if I stayed it would be in a position in which I was not truly wanted by the new owners and I could only foresee conflict in the weeks and months to come. I began to sense that the whole episode of the lesser position offered by Charles Church and the attractive one given to me by the Commander might well have been orchestrated. Indeed, I subsequently learnt that the Commander's son, Caspar, who had shot at Miltons in the past, had been lavish in his praise of my abilities and had specifically suggested to the Commander that I should be approached.

It also seems that my move had become general knowledge, in that on 19th January 1987 we hosted a 200-bird day at Miltons for a group of guns which included Peter Baxendale, who would later play an important role in developing shoot days at Castle Hill. Peter recorded in his diary that he found me something of a cheeky chap, especially because I had introduced the guns to a port-drinking game at the end of the day! He wrote: 'Brian is apparently going to Castle Hill – don't think he will last!'

In retrospect it does not really matter how and why I arrived at Castle Hill. I knew I was leaving Miltons and the Exmoor shoots with a reputation for being able to deliver high, challenging birds, which I would now have to extend and exceed. I was about to embark on my greatest challenge to date. I knew I now had a golden opportunity to develop Castle Hill into one of the world's greatest driven shoots.

CHAPTER FIVE

Castle Hill – A New Beginning

Angie and I said some very tearful goodbyes to our many friends at Miltons, and indeed across Exmoor, and made the short journey to our new life on the Castle Hill Estate. Our home, provided with the position, was, for the first six years, Winslade House. This was a rather 'back-sunned' house, where, due to its orientation, the sun was lost in November and only returned at the end of May. Naturally it was a very damp dwelling and it was with some relief that we eventually moved to our current home, a former cattle farm on the Estate. We consider ourselves so lucky to live where we do now. It is a lovely warm, sunny house, surrounded by simply beautiful scenery. Our large garden is cared for with great dedication by Angie and also we both have a passion for attracting wild birds to this lovely spot so plenty of feeders are scattered around. I always find it most amusing that the pheasants descend upon the garden, eating the wild bird food, from the 2nd February onwards. They certainly know when it is safe to show themselves!

The grounds of the Castle Hill Estate had been used for many years for game shooting. As a child, Lady Arran (the present incumbent) remembers Castle Hill as very much a family shoot, based around the house and on land much of which is now the Temple shoot. Bags of 200-bird days were the norm and the shooting was shared between a syndicate of local business gentlemen who were friends of Lady Arran's grandparents. When the present Lady Arran's mother, Lady Margaret Fortescue, came to Castle Hill, shooting continued in a similar vein, with forestry, for various tax reasons, being the mainstay of the Estate. Yet in 1988, with one stroke of his pen, the then Chancellor of the Exchequer, Nigel Lawson, removed many of the incentives for forestry development so that those running the Estate felt that alternative revenue streams should be explored. The re-letting of the shooting rights was one option considered, along with the commercial letting of the occasional day. In 1974 Lady Arran's uncle, Johnny Baxendale, had met Michael Rawlence in their club in London and mentioned to him that there might be an opportunity to gain syndicate shooting rights at Castle Hill. Michael jumped at this and rapidly assembled a team of guns, including Commander Sam MacDonald-Hall, who later took on the captaincy of the syndicate when Michael Rawlence fell on hard financial times. Although Michael's shooting at Castle Hill was before my time, his contribution to the success of the syndicate was recognised upon his death when both Lady Margaret and Lady Arran agreed that Michael's wishes should be followed: a simple ceremony was held on the Eggesford Bank drive, and his ashes scattered on one of the gun pegs.

Before my arrival Castle Hill had thus already acquired a good reputation as a first-class syndicate shoot, along with the adjoining Temple shoot, which for my first year was also under my remit. In the early years Commander MacDonald-Hall was my direct boss. Although Temple was, and is, a very good shoot, the topography of the Castle Hill shoot, the higher ground, meant that the drives on the latter were considered generally superior for very high birds. The Commander was, by this time, semi-retired and would fly down in his helicopter from his home in Essex on a fairly regular basis. I soon discovered that in his capacity as Shoot Captain the Commander's approach was to get involved with the day-to-day running of the shoot in some detail. I would even go so far as to say that his inclination was to micro-manage. I must admit that this took some getting used to after Alan Milton's relaxed approach.

Being the man I am, I was determined to make a great initial impression, right from the first day's shooting of the new season. This I was able to achieve on the Mays Quarry drive, when I managed to feed high quality birds, with just the right amount of spread and space between the flushes, over the gun line for more than an hour! All of the guns ran out of cartridges and we shot 380 birds on that one drive alone, a figure never achieved or even dreamed of on a drive at Castle Hill before. In retrospect, this is something I do not like to do too often, for a very high percentage of my birds were shot on this one drive: but it did achieve the aim of impressing the syndicate guns. On the other hand, this one drive also set a very high benchmark for me and raised everyone's expectations.

At the end of the drive I walked down to join the ecstatic guns, for I had been in the beating line, and was glad to receive their congratulations. I also made time to seek out the Commander, to receive his handshake, yes, but also to thank him for putting his trust in me. This drive was the beginning of an exceptional season and I took great pride in showing the syndicate higher birds than they had ever seen before at Castle Hill. I was also able to maintain high numbers right up until the end of January, whereas in the past, I understand, birds were often running out by Christmas.

I know that I am a difficult man to work with sometimes. I am a perfectionist and driven, occasionally, to the extreme. I am not a patient man either and always want to move forward. I was, most certainly back then, not typical of the average gamekeeper and I think several folk were wary of my reputation as something of a free spirit who possessed huge enthusiasm and energy. As usual, I threw myself wholeheartedly into my new role, wanting to change and alter things around as I saw fit. I did see it as my brief to produce fast, high quality birds. I believe, from what others have told me, that previously birds had often been pushed out from either halfway up a valley-side or a hill, or from even lower down. This is not how to produce high birds in my view and I would always (and still do today) try to push the birds from as high up a slope as possible, so as to show the challenging high birds for which Castle Hill has become so renowned. However, this technique did result in some moments of conflict with the Commander. I recall that we clashed on one particular occasion on the Deer Park drive, when he considered that the birds I was beginning to show in my first season were too high; he thought it would be best to move the guns further back, so as to shoot at the birds as they were descending. I refused to be persuaded on that one. However, despite my impatience, and almost psychotic drive, I was learning, and I did try to tread more carefully in my first few seasons. I even felt that occasionally I compromised, although others might not have seen things quite like that!

On my arrival I became aware that there was some suspicion, if not quite hostility, towards me from a few of the locals. Some folk are always going to be worried by change, and I suppose I represented change. As I say, there was no outright hostility, but in a way I would have preferred that because it is easier to deal with. The 'campaign' against me, if I can call it that, was more the case of a few people trying to undermine my authority and what I was trying to do. However, I was soon able to root out these few individuals and began to build up the great team that I now have around me. Of course this early period was a somewhat lonely one, but I did receive the help, support and advice of Gary Parsley, from the neighbouring Temple shoot, and he has remained a dear friend ever since.

In addition, I was able to bring across from Miltons three great stalwarts and friends. Brian Turner was soon leading the picking-up team, and continues to do so today. Despite my best efforts, Peter Gould insisted on following me and his loading skills and sense of fun and mischief have been a great asset to Castle Hill and – usually – appreciated by me. Finally, Nigel Brimacombe, who loaded for me at Miltons, also came across to Castle Hill. Nigel, who very sadly was claimed by cancer a few years ago, was a great friend of Peter's and a dairy farmer from Yeoford, where he also ran a very good family shoot. Both the farm and shoot have remained in the family and Nigel's wife Marion and son Paul, with his wife Claire, now continue both enterprises. Since Nigel's death the Brimacombe family have become even greater friends and each year my wife Angie and I travel to Yeoford for the family Christmas shoot, which is a lovely, relaxed day out.

Of course I must never forget to emphasise the wonderful help and support given to me by Angie, and this is probably as good a moment as any to acknowledge her great contribution to the work that I do and also to the happiness of our life together. Not only has she been there to listen to my moans and groans, and to absorb all the stresses and strains of my job, but on a practical level she has been, and remains, an important part of the picking-up team too. Until recently she also processed much of the shoot day admin, such as beaters' wages, as well as dealing so efficiently and uncomplainingly with all the mysteries of end-of-year P60s and other bureaucracy. I personally could not have achieved what I have at Castle Hill without Angie by my side: I know that I am a very lucky man.

Once at Castle Hill, I learnt that a certain reputation had followed me from Miltons. Quite what that reputation was, I never really grasped for sure. I suppose I had had a great deal of freedom at Miltons to change and improve things as I chose for the shoots I had under my charge. I can understand that to some people the direct approach that I favoured might have been viewed as perhaps being a bit dictatorial, or even that I was something of a loose cannon. Either way, the jungle drums had beaten and news of my 'reputation', whatever it was, did indeed follow me. Yet I also wanted to show that I could be conciliatory and this was reflected in a discussion with one of the forestry workers soon after I arrived. I learnt that this individual very much liked to take his dog with him while working in the woods. This had been a significant area of conflict with the previous keeper, who had been adamant that this should not be permitted. Having myself gained such pleasure from having a dog by my side during my working day, I certainly was not going to deprive the forester of this – much, I think, to his surprise.

In defence of my rather direct approach, it has to be acknowledged that I was in something of a new working environment, in which I would have several elements to consider, with the syndicate and the working of the Estate at the heart of my thinking. I freely admit that trying to distinguish between the sometimes opposing concerns was difficult at times. This is perhaps best illustrated by an early encounter I had with the Estate's land agent, Hugh Thomas.

Our first, and only significant, clash in twenty-five years came when on my own initiative, and entirely for the benefit of the shoot, I felled some trees on one of the plantations without consulting Hugh or anyone else. Hugh, it seemed, decided to take the opportunity to put me in my place. I was summoned to his office and, in front of Lady Arran, I was severely, and perhaps rather unkindly, given a dressing-down. I suppose it was important to him to lay down some boundaries early on in our relationship, and the incident also allowed him to demonstrate how tough a land agent could be in front of his employer. I must say that I found the experience very awkward, especially as I felt that I had been acting with the best of intentions. Throughout the meeting I was determined to remain dignified and not confrontational. At the conclusion of Hugh's rant I did explain that the five or six trees that had been felled were in the line of sight of the guns and had been removed so as to improve that particular drive. I was sure that Hugh knew that I had been acting with the best of intentions for the shoot. From then on, I began to understand that although the shoot was an important component of Castle Hill, it was just one of the elements that made the Estate successful and that a team approach was, and is, vital. I am delighted to say that from that moment on Hugh and I became firm friends, with a real working understanding.

Soon after my arrival, and following many years of discussion, a decision was finally made to re-route the A361 road, which ran in front of the Castle Hill gate house. The road had become inadequate for the amount of traffic that it was then carrying. The choice was made that the new road should largely follow the route of the old North Devon railway and so the North Devon Link Road was constructed a couple of miles behind the Castle Hill main house. Fortunately its route utilised some of the flattest ground on the Estate and as such did not affect any major drives directly, but the road's construction did have a number of implications for the shoot and the local wildlife. In the first year of the new road's existence I do remember that pest control was made easier: the foxes tended to congregate in a specific area near the Deer Park drive, for it seemed that the road had confused them and they were unsure of their bearings. Similarly, many more badgers and deer appeared on shoot ground and, sadly, several deer were run over trying to cross an obstacle that had not previously been part of their normal deer-runs.

Although we lost some acreage to the road, initially there was little impact on the shoot itself as our pens were located far enough away. Indeed, we were fortunate in that the Estate did receive some compensation from the Department of Transport for the link road being built on its land and we were able to direct some of this money towards the development of other drives. However, as the shoot expanded, increasingly pheasants began to find their way on to the road, with predictable results.

I hate to see dead birds littering the road. Some years are worse than others: wetter seasons seem to make the birds wander more and the 'body count' on the road reflects this. Those that are hit to the side of the road, on or beyond the white tramlines, can stay there for weeks and in my view such a sight reflects badly on shooting as a whole. The road is now so busy, and thus dangerous, that I would never inflict this task on anyone else but I will, when required, venture on to the North Devon Link Road to remove the carcases. This grisly job has to be undertaken at three a.m. when I feel that the risk to life and limb is minimised! Tragically, the road has claimed many other victims and during my sorties I have removed five dead otters, as well as barn owls and numerous badgers, foxes and deer.

After a number of years as a beat-keeper at Chargot, my eldest son, Robert, decided that he needed a change and moved out of the industry to try other things. He spent some time working as a garage mechanic and a plasterer. I had been at Castle Hill for about a year when I wondered whether Robert could be persuaded back into the world of shooting and I offered him some casual labouring work around the shoot. When we discovered that we could work together without killing each other, I offered Robert a position of beat-keeper that had become vacant. He agreed to give it a go and we managed to work alongside each other for six years. I can't say our time was always harmonious, and I know I can be a bit of a bugger to work for, but in retrospect our time together was productive and I know Robert found the company of his fellow beat-keepers, the likes of Peter Hewitt and Gary Liddle, to be enjoyable. I would like to stress that although Robert's appointment could be seen to be a case of nepotism, in reality it was not. I offered Robert the job based solely on his own merits, for I knew he could handle it admirably, which of course he did. He had responsibility for the drives in the Tordown and Riverton valleys and he spent much of his time clearing the land and valley bottoms of brambles so as to really open up and develop the drives there.

Unfortunately our working relationship came to something of a bitter end one spring day, when I returned from holiday in something of a bad mood and quickly found fault with the work Robert and the other beat-keepers had done to build a pen for the Lane drive. The lads had been building the pen in the snow for the previous ten days and were probably not in the mood for my ranting. Anyway, it was not great timing on my part and Robert decided to walk. Luckily, however, he has gone on to great success as Head Keeper at North Molton and I am very proud of what he has achieved there. Our relationship has recovered and developed and we are now as close as we have ever been.

The Commander was now in his early seventies and I do think he struggled somewhat to connect with the higher birds. Whilst I am sure that the younger syndicate members approved of what I was trying to achieve, I will not deny that there was an element of conflict between the Commander and me. This was tragically resolved when in 1990 Commander MacDonald-Hall was killed in a helicopter crash. This was a very sad end to an extraordinary life and, although we may not have seen eye-to-eye on a few occasions, I had huge respect for him. His death was a sad loss for both his family and the Castle Hill syndicate.

Within days of the Commander's accident I received a telephone call from his son, Caspar MacDonald-Hall, who phoned to reassure me about two things, my position and the syndicate's intention of maintaining and developing the shoot. This was very welcome news and it was a huge personal relief for me that I had the support of the syndicate members. These then included Michael Rivkin, Alan Elliot and John and Michael Chandris. I travelled to

Essex with Alan Sexon to attend the Commander's funeral and we were able to place a number of pheasant tail-feathers in his grave, as a mark of the respect we all felt for him.

I would like to state that working for the syndicate, alongside its administrator, Val Woulf, has been a real pleasure. Over the years, all the members of the syndicate, who have not altered dramatically, have been very supportive of my attempts to improve various drives and introduce new ones. They have backed me on the rare occasion a sensitive issue has had to be resolved and have been generous in supporting me when my health or body, such as my knee-joints, has had to be fixed. Val in particular has been generous with her time and good advice and has enabled me to grasp the financial details and running of the shoot. What has been achieved at Castle Hill has been through a real team effort and the syndicate members have played a major part in this success.

Thus, following the Commander's tragic death and in only my fourth season at the Estate, I found myself working for a new boss, Caspar MacDonald-Hall. This season also saw a significant change in my role. Apparently the future of shooting on the Estate had received much consideration from Lady Margaret, Lady Arran and the land agent, Hugh Thomas. Whilst there was agreement that the Castle Hill shoot should be encouraged to continue in its present form, and even expand, there was a desire that the Temple shoot be let to a local syndicate of businessmen and that it should, at that time, withdraw somewhat from large, commercially-let days. To my surprise and delight I was told that the new Temple syndicate was to be led by my old boss Alan Milton, which just goes to show what a small, incestuous world shooting sometimes is. The Head Keeper at Bulland, Mark Atkinson, again someone I had previously worked alongside, was enticed to the Temple shoot and he has remained there ever since, working first of all for Alan, then Dick Cawthorne and now Gary Parsley, who was an original member of the Miltons syndicate. Temple produces high quality syndicate shooting, with the occasional let day every season. Naturally I was disappointed to lose control of such quality drives as Temple and Meadow Park, but I completely understood the logic behind the split and I realised that I would now have more time and opportunity to concentrate on how to expand and improve the Castle Hill shoot.

There were several very obvious changes that I felt had to be made so as to improve the quality of the birds quickly. One was to move away from the rearing of our own birds (more on this in the next chapter), and the second was to expand the ground over which we were to shoot. I repeated my old Exmoor trick and drove around the edges of the Estate to look at likely ground into which we might be able to expand. I then approached the local farmers: men like John and Bert Bartlett, George Snell and Andrew Down all received the Mitchell knock on their front doors, and, with a bit of persuasion, the shoot acreage began to increase. I first met Alan Sexon, who has since become a great and dear friend, when I approached him to increase the size of the cover-crop plot at Yollacombe, to which he agreed.

The wonderful topography in and around the Castle Hill Estate would, I knew, allow me to introduce many new stunning drives, but we were also able, with the later assistance of Hugh Thomas, to gain shooting rights over both sides of the river valleys. In my early years I would come knocking on his office door, with a map of the Estate in hand and I would indicate to Hugh that I strongly felt that certain terrain or areas on either the Estate land, or adjacent tenanted farms, could be made into successful, even superlative, drives. Hugh immediately grasped my thinking and I am sure he was just as excited as I was at the prospect of developing and extending the Castle Hill shoot.

Ownership, or tenancy, boundaries frequently cut along river valleys meaning that we would often have to negotiate with two individuals in order to shoot successfully in such locations. Although this could on occasion be somewhat time-consuming, the results, such as the establishment of the Sandy Park drive and more recently Kite's Nest, were certainly worth all the effort. The ability to fly birds from one side of a valley to the other added a new, exciting, and challenging aspect to the Castle Hill shoot. Of course such developments did not happen overnight and several years passed before we were able to increase the total acreage over which we shoot at Castle Hill by over 1,000 acres to our current total of around 9,000 acres. With the increase in acreage came a corresponding increase in the number of birds.

Of course a great deal of effort goes into developing a new drive. First the terrain and suitability of the land has to be identified. I was particularly drawn to the Riverton valley and it did not take me long to see the possibilities of what were to become the Collythorne and the Toredown drives. Close by is Tadiport Lane, and by obtaining shooting rights in this area too we were able to establish a release pen area to feed these new drives, as well as Accott, and, on the other side of the valley, Mill and Buckland drives. I am fortunate that I have the luxury of being able to experiment with new drives on the syndicate guns first, who are always receptive to the idea of trying new drives. Only then, if a drive works, and they don't always, will it become a Castle Hill drive and be available to all who shoot with us.

If the area happens to be on ground adjacent to the Estate, then shooting rights and rights of access have to be obtained from landowners and farmers and annual rental terms have to be negotiated and agreed. Once all this has been achieved, decisions need to be made as to where to site and build release pens and where to plant cover crops. The type of crops that will work best in specific soils or with the prevailing winds also needs some serious consideration. As I have already mentioned, the whole process takes a great deal of time and effort and it is rare to get everything right the first time. From a negotiating point of view this can, and has been, rather frustrating; for having agreed with landowners and tenants which areas the shoot would like to use for cover crops or release pens, sometimes after the first year of use, we would have to go back to the negotiating table and obtain rights over slightly different areas.

Having said all that, many of our negotiating sessions, particularly with the tenant farmers, were highly enjoyable. Much of what Hugh and I achieved were deals done in farmers' kitchens; hours would be spent in discussions about land use and rental agreements with these savvy farmers, who knew that they were in a fairly strong negotiating position. We were fortunate in that with the support and backing of the syndicate we were, and still are, able to offer a significant financial incentive to farmers at a good rate per acre. The rent is the same whether the land is for shooting over, for a release pen or for a cover crop. To have a reliable source of income during a period of the year when the farm is frequently fairly dormant is attractive to many. In addition I was keen, right from the start, to make the rental payment sufficient to compensate the landowner or tenant for any disruption to their daily working lives, caused by thousands of pheasants on their land or shoot vehicles increasing the traffic on narrow, rural roads. Many were the times, in those early years, when the consumption of a bottle of whisky eased our discussions far more than the talk of rent to be earned and produced the right agreements to suit the farmer, the shoot and the Estate.

However, some farmers and landowners, even those on land over which the Estate had legal shooting rights, could never be persuaded. Whatever their reasons, Hugh and I had to respect their decisions and move on elsewhere. It was never our intention or remit to force shooting upon folk who simply did not agree with it or did not want it on their land and we tried to accept such decisions with good grace, though perhaps with more than a little frustration.

Understandably, working as we do with a bird that does like to wander, likes to peck under hedges and sometimes eat crops that it is not meant to, a few issues have arisen between the shoot and neighbouring landowners over the past twenty-five years or so. It would be a miracle if we had not had the odd occasion on which a complaint has been made. On these, fortunately rare, occasions, I have always made a point of going to see the farmer concerned myself and at once, so as to address the problem immediately. I also prefer to offer to do any remedial work myself, or arrange for someone to do it, for I think this demonstrates the shoot's commitment to making sure that our working relationships continue as harmoniously as possible. Similarly, our policy of capturing birds at the end of the season, although driven primarily by the essential need to give the ground a rest, does have the added benefit of allowing farmers who have had to put up with the birds on their land a break from the pressures and demands that that level of density of birds can inflict.

In the early days, these rental negotiations allowed me to show my face in the locality, meet folk and in many instances make lifelong friendships. I was keen to make as much use as possible of the local pool of (soon to become) willing folk. In my first year I became an enthusiastic member of the local skittles team, which met regularly in the Old Rectory in Filleigh. Locals such as Alan Sexon, Mike Buckley, Alec Facey and John Cook were members of the team and still are today. I had realised that I needed to increase the pool of loaders at Castle Hill for the forthcoming season, so the night before our next skittles session I phoned around my team-mates and, without explanation, told each to arrive an hour early and to bring his shotgun with him. All duly obeyed my request and I soon had them lined up in the skittles alley as I demonstrated the art and skill of becoming a competent loader. We had a few laughs and several mistakes were made but it didn't take long for several of them to become reliable loaders in their own right.

I can remember the bemused looks I had received from my colleagues when I told them of my plan: they must have thought I was slightly mad. Yet I was able to bring these folk along with me in my 'mad' but exciting plan to make Castle Hill *the* best shoot – which meant that everything had to be perfect. Some of the tenant farmers, such as Brian Latham and Graham Macleod, also joined my loading team, and became first-class loaders and very good friends too. They were, and still are, dedicated to their shooting profession. They all have a commitment to Castle Hill that goes way beyond the payment of a few pounds, a free lunch and a walk in the countryside. I sincerely believe that these good folk, these real professionals, are proud of the part they have played in the development and the success of our shoot, whether they be loaders, pickers-up or beaters. Because of this they turn out in all weathers, come wind, rain or shine, and do a superb job.

Of course extra shooting land meant an increase in the number of birds, something which the syndicate actively encouraged. Indeed, with the rise in prominence of the nearby North Molton shoot, which put down significantly more birds than we used to, Castle Hill found that it needed to raise its numbers so as to maintain and expand upon our commercially let days. We were beginning to find that the gun who travelled to Castle Hill, many of whom came from great distances, were enthralled by the quality and challenging nature of our birds but were looking for bigger and bigger bags, something that North Molton could provide. No longer could we send a dozen quality birds over each peg in a drive, for our commercial clients were now looking to see hundreds of birds in the sky and expecting 500-bird days even at the end of January. Such figures could only be achieved with an increase in numbers and in acreage. However, our ambitions were restricted by the shooting tenancy that the syndicate then had with the Castle Hill Estate, which limited the number of birds put down to 50,000. Around eight years ago, realising that the demands of shooting were changing, Caspar MacDonald-Hall approached the Estate's trustees with a request to increase this number. After some discussions, the syndicate did finally gain approval for a significant rise and we are now able to offer more than sixty 500-bird days a season. Of course these numbers do present their own issues, but now we are confident that we are able to give the syndicate guns and our visiting clients the days they are expecting.

With the encouragement of the syndicate, in the early years I was not only looking to increase the shoot's acreage, the number of birds and the number of drives, but I also looked at the existing drives with a fresh pair of eyes. Lady Arran once told me that my arrival brought a new energy to the shoot and everyone, especially me, was always in a great hurry to get to places, to drive the shoot forward. Whilst some of the existing drives did offer great shooting I could frequently see that with a few alterations they could be improved further, so as to offer even more challenging birds. Indeed, with a large increase in cover-crop planting and bigger release pens, I can honestly say that all the drives I inherited when I first arrived at Castle Hill have been altered and improved considerably.

I have already mentioned the Deer Park drive and how by launching the birds from the top of the hill their height and difficulty was increased considerably. Of course this was not the only secret to improving that particular drive. I planted laurels and a large area of maize, as well as long-term cover such as miscanthus grass, to provide warm shelter for the birds. I also learnt what climatic conditions work best for this drive. For example, a cold easterly wind will mean that the birds will not fly higher than the tree-tops on Deer Park. Years ago, the drive would have been shot on many more days than it is now, simply because it was such an accepted part of the Castle Hill day but also because the shoot had far fewer drives from which to choose. Now I have the luxury of being able to shoot this drive, and the other thirty or so at my disposal, when the weather conditions suit them best.

Another drive that I felt could be improved upon was Bury Knoll, which had always been driven so that the birds came out of the bottom of the wood. Early in my tenure I changed this approach and took the birds out of the top of the drive. I received some criticism for this from one or two of the syndicate guns as they were concerned that I would adversely affect what was already a great drive. Despite the opposition, I dug my heels in, for I was convinced that once I and the beating team had established exactly how to beat the drive, and what climatic and atmospheric conditions favoured the drive best, we could transform the quality of the birds it produced. It took one or two seasons to perfect the technique as to how and when to beat the drive, but many now consider Bury Knoll the pinnacle of drives at Castle Hill for offering high, fast, challenging birds.

Similarly, I have always felt that every drive should be constantly re-evaluated. The ground does change, after all. Trees grow and trees die, and such natural events can drastically alter a drive for better or worse: any effects need to be assessed, as does the type of cover crop used. Although maize is preferred by many gamekeepers, I have found to my cost at Castle Hill that our climate means that in some wet summers it just does not thrive. Therefore I have frequently introduced a back-up cover crop such as laurel, which, with a healthy showering of corn, will attract the birds and keep them in the warm surroundings. Also, just because a new drive has been working well, it does not mean that it can't be improved further. For example, the introduction of the Brayley drive in my early years had been well received, but I felt that it had yet to reach its full potential. I deduced that the release pen needed to be relocated and enlarged. This simple measure utterly transformed the drive and now many guns, loaders and beaters consider Brayley to be their particular favourite.

Although I now have three beat-keepers working under me, each with the responsibility for their own drives in terms of feeding and maintenance and so on, I still look after some drives myself. I am up every morning at the crack of dawn to feed the birds in the valley near my house, which includes such drives as the Punch Bowl and Brayley. I am not sure how many Head Keepers do this, perhaps preferring extra time in bed, but I find this first hour of the day not only strangely relaxing and calming, but also it gives me some vital information about the health and well-being of the birds and, if it is a shoot day, I can gain some important clues as to how the day will go.

When I was at the height of my responsibilities at Miltons, supervising other shoots like Chargot as well, I was simply too busy to have this early morning time on the land. My job was so broad and I usually spent the early hours of a shoot day with the guns, which, although important, did perhaps take my eye away from the vital ingredients for a successful day's shooting. I was then, and most certainly am now, first and foremost a gamekeeper: the priority should always be the responsibility of looking after the game itself. That aspect of the job has always been and will remain my first love. Being on the land, feeling that I am close to nature is so, so important to me. What is also important to me is that I have been able to move out of the beating line, although I was there in my first couple of years at Castle Hill, and I now stand behind the gun line on each drive.

This was considered fairly revolutionary when I first decided to take this step back, but I would now strongly argue that on any big-bag days, on any shoot, the Head Keeper really needs to be out front, standing just behind the gun line, so that he can constantly assess the drive and see exactly how the birds are flying over it. From there one can easily judge how the driving is working – in terms of assessing the wind, air pressure and so on – and how it is being, and perhaps needs to be, beaten. A few quick words on the radio will alter the beating line and ensure that the drive is managed to the best of all our abilities for the enjoyment and satisfaction of the guns. A shouted command at precisely the right moment for the beating line to fall to the ground so that no one is visible, or, alternatively for those in the line to unfurl and wave their flags to keep birds back just when they might be considering sneaking out of the side of a drive, is something I have learnt from years of experience or possibly it is an instinct that I inherently possess.

We have all seen drives where perhaps the guns on pegs one and two get the majority of the shooting whilst those at the other end of the line have a very sparse drive. Alternatively, birds might be fairly mediocre over one part of the line and spectacular over another. I am ultimately trying to achieve high, challenging birds in sufficient numbers over the whole of the gun line, from numbers one to eight. This aim is not always achieved but I try to ensure that the amount and quality of shooting is spread as evenly as possible. In my experience guns do not like to move once on their pegs, so it is up to me and the beat-keepers to make the necessary adjustments during the drive.

I suppose by positioning myself where I do, I am able to gauge things from the pheasant's perspective. I can readily use the radio to keep in touch with the beat-keepers and beaters throughout a drive and I suppose my years of experience mean that I do seem to know instinctively what the birds are thinking, and where they are going – perhaps even before the birds know themselves!

My man-management skills might be considered rudimentary at best by some of the beat-keepers I have employed. The four keepers who currently work under me (in 2014), Alex Brine, Stuart Walker, Gareth De Rusett and Ed Northcote, all of whom are local lads, will probably agree with that statement: yet little do they know that I have mellowed! No, I don't always communicate my views or intentions for the day very effectively, and yes, I have been known to lose my temper on more than one occasion, yet in my defence, I would say that running a shoot day at somewhere like Castle Hill is a large and difficult operation, which can be incredibly stressful and provides numerous opportunities for disasters and cock-ups. Someone once described a shoot day as something of a powder keg that is ready to explode: not a bad description. Not only are the keepers attempting to produce success in placing high birds in sufficiently large numbers over waiting guns, they are also having to contain and cope with some big, and often competing, personalities. This is why having the right team of beaters, keepers and pickers-up is vital. Having said that, it is rare for errors to occur on my shoot; I put some of this success down to my obsessive approach, my determination and my micro-management style, which in the circumstances I have described is what I believe is required. I can understand that such a managerial approach might not always be appreciated, but I, and the shooting at Castle Hill, are judged by successful results and success does not happen by chance or a relaxed stance. I know that I can, sometimes, be a 'bear with a sore head', but I also realise when I have overstepped the mark and if I have, I do not hesitate to apologise. I may be many things to many people on a shoot day, but I do try my level best to be fair. I would like to be regarded by folk as a fair-minded person, although I readily admit that I might not always be viewed as such.

I have on very rare occasions, perhaps only twice in twenty-five years, 'pulled' or stopped a drive and moved on to the next. When this has happened I have taken the time to explain to the guns that the adverse natural conditions have meant the birds are not flying well and are not what we would consider good enough to be classed as Castle Hill birds. I really do not like to do this for it is in a sense admitting defeat and I am reluctant to leave birds in drives. I would rather end what is becoming an average drive with a flourish and flush out the remaining birds. The code word for the beat-keepers is 'jam jar', basically meaning opening the jar lid so to speak, to release its contents. When I utter these words those in the beating line know to let their dogs off their leads and rush through the rest of the drive. This produces a huge flush of birds, which is in itself a spectacular end to a drive and at least allows the guns the fun of seeing large numbers of birds in the air. I know many keepers, including my son, do not see the point of emptying the drive of birds in such a fashion, arguing that it only risks the birds being sent to where they should not be. However, I see such a 'spectacular' as being a good way to get reluctant birds to fly and, as I have said, it ends a slightly disappointing drive with an unforgettable sight for the guns.

During almost fifty years of being a gamekeeper I have

naturally acquired a great deal of experience. This has led me to determine four major signs that do not bode well for a successful day's shooting, as they will detrimentally influence how the birds will fly. The first is noticeable in the morning when I go out early to feed: if there is cold, heavy air on my cheeks, I know that the atmospheric pressure in low and that this will stop the birds flying high. Secondly, when the first shot of the day is fired, if the sound that this blast makes is a 'thud' as opposed to a 'ring', then I again know that the atmospheric pressure will be an issue. The third indicator, again related to air pressure, is when the first pheasant is shot dead in the air and the feathers that come out of the bird just hang slowly in the air rather than drifting straight down. The final sign is whether you can smell the gunpowder from your neighbour's gun. If you can, then this illustrates that the smoke and vapours from the cartridge are not going up into the air, but that the air pressure is such that this distinctive smell lingers rather than rising upwards.

If these four indicators are present, the main thing is not to panic. The air pressure can alter very rapidly and what looks like a difficult day's shooting can suddenly change. For example, towards the end of the 2014 season, we had one let day when in the morning the air pressure was heavy and the birds, despite our best efforts, flew very poorly. I was disappointed for the guns and the Estate because we had been unable to show the birds for which Castle Hill is so renowned. There were some grumblings over lunch! However, as we left the shooting lodge I quickly perceived that the pressure had risen considerably. The afternoon drives were spectacular and certainly made up for the disappointment of the morning. Furthermore, the last drive benefited from what I call the 'golden moment', which is just before a large amount of rainfall, or a heavy shower. Don't ask me to explain the physics behind this, but this small window before the rain arrives lifts the air pressure significantly and the birds fly even higher. As I said, on this day the 'golden moment' coincided with our last drive of the day and I have never seen the birds fly as well there. Phew! Happy and content, the guns departed, but not before booking again for next year. I suppose the one thing I have definitely learnt from my years of gamekeeping is that, despite everything that is done to either nullify or enhance its effects, the day's shooting is ultimately dependent on nature and all that it has to offer.

There are some basic weather conditions that I think all keepers will know are either good or bad on a shoot day. A low winter sun, for example, will make both partridge and pheasant try to escape its dazzling rays by 'flying under the sun' and the birds will have no height. It is also important to have an understanding, at some basic level, of the science of how a pheasant flies and the restrictions placed upon the bird by its physiology. A pheasant, particularly a large, heavy cock bird, is not exactly aerodynamic and I like to think of them as land-lovers who will just about take off if threatened. The burst of energy at take-off can last for only about eight seconds and this is due to the fact that a pheasant has a very weak supply of blood to its main flight muscles. (Evidence of this limited blood-flow is the pale meat on the bird's breast.) This physical constraint needs to be understood and considered when devising drives and placing guns, for the aim is for the birds still to be rising over the gun line, not descending.

On every shoot day I have in my wallet a list of all the drives with details of how to beat them, depending on the wind direction as well as its strength. Some drives will produce stunning birds in a gale but generally the birds will dip to avoid the worst of the wind. Of course, I will also take into consideration on the day whether it is raining, sunny, frosty, even snowing, as well as the, potentially, dreaded atmospheric pressure before deciding which drive to beat next. I know this can, on occasions, be frustrating to both the guns and my beat-keepers, as I suddenly turn my Land Rover around and head in the opposite direction to the one everyone was expecting, barking out a change of drive on my radio. I also expect, and know, that when we get there the beaters and stops will already be in place, like the professionals that they are. Never do we have a day at Castle Hill when all four or six drives are pre-determined at the start of the day with that choice being adhered to rigorously. We simply do not work like that, but will always be looking and assessing to make sure that we shoot the best drives available for the conditions on the day. If we end up shooting the same drive on consecutive days then we will, if that produces the best birds. Indeed, we have even been known to shoot the same drive at the start and the end of the day, although this is rare: but if I know that this is where the best, most challenging birds are to be found then I won't hesitate to make that call.

Of course assessing conditions is not just about showing the best birds, but also avoiding sending pheasants over the guns that are too easy! Again, I have learnt that if a bird is driven very straight with the wind behind it, then it can't gain the benefit of the air pressure to both lift it higher and give it some drift. As a consequence it becomes an average bird for Castle Hill and is readily, and too easily, dispatched by the guns that shoot there. The best winds I look for are those coming from the side, from the beaters to the guns. This allows the birds to lift, drift, slide and even quarter in the wind, increasing both their height and speed and thus making them very challenging birds to shoot. If, however, the wind is coming at a cross-angle, from the guns back towards the drive, then it will be very detrimental, for the pheasant will not be able to fly very fast. With the vagaries of wind speed and direction it is not always possible to judge its effects until the drive is under way, and of course wind direction can, and does, change during a drive. Standing behind the guns as I do, I can readily assess the wind's impact too and can contact the beat-keepers via the radio so that the beating line can be altered accordingly. I will delay the start of a drive if it is sunny, but only if I can see that cloud is approaching and that the sun will soon be covered. Although the delay might sometimes be frustrating for the guns, it is common knowledge that pheasants do not fly as well in bright sunshine and if a short delay can reduce the adverse effects of sunshine then I will wait.

The radio also allows me to control the use of flags amongst the beating line. I would readily admit that if a bird has made up its mind and set its wings then no amount of flagging will alter its direction. However, I, perhaps more than any other keeper in Britain, place a huge amount of importance on the correct and timely use of flags during a drive. I frequently line up beaters along the side of a drive, whether that be a cover-crop or wood, and as the drive progresses I will instruct them to move their flags constantly. This does not mean that the flags are being waved frantically above heads, but often are just being held down by the waist and gently shaken. The movement and the noise that this generates is, I believe, just enough to keep a bird that might be thinking of slipping out of the side of the drive firmly within it. Alternatively, if a drive is not going quite to plan, I will tell the beaters on the side to lie flat on the ground so that their profiles cannot be seen by the birds. I then instruct the back line to move into the drive, to push any birds who were thinking of trying to escape out of the back or side to either stay put or move forwards. All this can happen very quickly and a drive can be ruined in a matter of seconds, particularly towards the end of the season when the birds are more experienced and jumpy. However, I am confident that with the team we have at Castle Hill we put as high a percentage of available birds over the guns as anywhere else.

If the birds are reacting well to the wind and are sliding and drifting in the air, then it can make them out of reach for many teams of guns. It takes many years of shooting at such birds for a gun to perceive the sometimes very slight sideways movement as a bird flies towards them and for them to alter their aim accordingly. For some teams this is the kind of challenge they are seeking. For others, being under such birds can be disheartening, even soul-destroying. This is when I have to look at and assess the team's body language and if the guns are clearly not enjoying the

The Bury Knoll drive – on its day this drive produces the highest birds at Castle Hill

Above: The Brayley drive, with the North Devon highway in the background

Below: The Proutworthy drive in the snow – this is my main east wind drive

Below right: The Mill drive – a warm-up drive to get the guns in the mood to expect more!

Left: The Colythorn drive – another high bird drive…with the right cartridges, and the correct level of skill, birds can be cleanly dispatched

Above: One of the most important jobs on a shoot day – recording the 'cartridge to kill ratio' which I do after each drive

Below: The Mays Quarry drive – a spectacular vista of my most reliable drive at Castle Hill

Smoldon's Bottom – the birds zip out over the conifers and this produces some very difficult shooting. Our record of cartridges on this drive stands at 2,670!

Left: Another high bird cleanly dispatched on the Deer Park drive

Above: Me in the background, with radio in hand, carefully watching and directing proceedings

Below: The Deer Park drive – one of the oldest drives at Castle Hill and, for many of our guns, the best

The Eggesford Bank drive – this drive produces some wonderfully high birds, especially after Christmas

Above: The Team (or most of them anyway)! Without their efforts and commitment the day at Castle Hill would just not be possible

Left: Yollacombe – this is a great drive with a south westerly wind

Below: It is not all stress – me sharing a joke with one of the guns

Above: The Annual Boxing Day Shoot – a great time to get together. Me with my son, Robert, and his three children, Hugo, Harriet and Gracie

Left: Angie, my wonderful wife, whose help and support has been so crucial to our success at Castle Hill

Below: Our pickers-up and their dogs do a fantastic job

experience I instruct my beat-keepers to beat the birds so that they take off lower down the slope and thus do not gain the full benefit of height or drift. To stress, or perhaps over-stress, the point, such a judgement comes from experience!

One tool that I use to either spur guns on or perhaps even bring them down a peg if they are shooting too well, is to pick a suitable outstandingly high bird and shout 'Fiver!' All the guns have been briefed at the start of the day that if I shout this and the bird is killed in the air, I personally will pay the successful gun five pounds from my own pocket, which I will sign, date and write on the name of the drive. As you can imagine, I select the birds carefully, or else I would be a poor man! Yet I am happy to pay out on occasion and last season paid out twice on the same drive to the same gun, Alan Perrin. Alan was so pleased with this achievement that he had the fivers framed and they are in pride of place in our shoot room.

Shoot days can be incredibly stressful and as I speed around the Estate I usually share my vehicle with some of the loaders, such as Peter Gould and Phil Lay, who know when to take the mickey out of me so as to reduce my stress levels. The Land Rover is full of laughter despite the fact that I am desperately trying to assess the weather and other factors before deciding on which drive to do next. Peter Gould will frequently slip the Land Rover out of gear or ratio when I am not looking, which I find infuriating, but it breaks the tension sometimes. Likewise, if we have to turn vehicles around, I am always the lead vehicle and have to pass the one that contains the other loaders, usually driven by Alan Sexon. It has become a tradition to try to spray one another with bottled water as we pass. Silly I know, but stress-relieving too. Peter also has a habit of dismantling a cartridge and placing the lead shot into folks' boots during lunch and this all adds to the general level of fun on a day.

One saying that materialised at the end of last season came about when Phil Lay asked me what drive we would be shooting next, just as I was peering out of the window with one eye on the road and the other on the sky. I responded to Phil's perfectly valid question by rather briskly replying, 'We're doing the No-f******-idea drive next!' Naturally this answer was greeted with hoots of derision by my passengers, which broke the tense mood into which I had cast myself. The concept of the 'No-f******-idea drive' has now entered into folklore and I am sure it is a phrase that will be repeated many times over the coming seasons! Although this story is somewhat crude it does illustrate that we very rarely have a set plan on a shoot day. I will simply go where the best birds are to be found on the day, based on the conditions.

Managing the day and managing the team of guns are my biggest challenges. The syndicate days and the sold commercial days are two very different things. Whilst I think I know the syndicate guns pretty well and am able to share a drink and a laugh with them, I also know that I must be respectful and that my prime job is to challenge them constantly with high, demanding birds. This is why they shoot at Castle Hill. I am also aware that the syndicate guns like a fresh challenge, which is why I am always looking to alter and improve existing drives and even introduce new ones. The Kite's Nest drive was established only in the last three seasons and, although already offering exceptional shooting, I am sure it has not yet reached its full potential. This drive has already become a firm favourite with the syndicate. At the other extreme are the commercially let days. Whilst many of our guns are regulars and have shot at Castle Hill on several occasions, others have not. At the start of the day's shooting I have to assess the guns quickly as to their ability levels, as well as gain an understanding of what the team want from the day. This can be difficult as it is often the case that individuals in a team have competing views. Whilst one person may be happy to fire hundreds of cartridges and be thrilled by bringing down a small number of quality high birds that they will remember forever, others want the bag size that they have paid for and expect to be given birds that are within their abilities to hit. Thus it can be extremely difficult to manage such a day and manage everyone's expectations.

I have sometimes been known to take a rather direct approach. One thing I pride myself on is that I can usually assess folk quite quickly and know whether individuals or a team will be more open to a few laughs or mickey-taking than others. One person with whom I had an instant rapport was a gentleman named Simon Ford, who shot at Castle Hill for the first time six seasons ago, bringing with him a competent team of guns including Ian Musto. I made a point of visiting the team at a nearby hotel, Northcote Manor, where they had stayed for the night before the shoot day. I introduced myself at breakfast. I could feel that the team was excited, and perhaps a little nervous about the day, but I could also sense that they had a real desire to enjoy themselves, an attitude that I love and appreciate. There was also plenty of humour in the air. Simon asked me what the team could expect. This was my cue! I made myself fairly plain when I replied, 'I am going to put some birds over you, you are going to fire three thousand shots between you and not hit any of my birds; that's the objective for the day!' I had laid down the gauntlet. I started this new team on the Deer Park drive. With a strong sideways wind, just the kind I love, the birds were sixty to eighty yards up, sliding and curling. I later learnt that Ian Musto fired twenty-eight shots before he managed to touch so much as a feather! Despite the difficulties the team were experiencing I could sense that they were loving every minute and I resolved to show them even more testing birds. Their day included the Brayley, Punchbowl and Colythorn drives and ended with all the guns saying that it was the best day they had ever experienced. Although I managed to beat them on that first occasion, Simon and his team have been back to Castle Hill many times since and I can honestly say that I enjoy their days as much as they do. All, incidentally, can now hit my birds! As I say, shoot technique is all about getting to know the team of guns, their abilities and expectations, and then trying to exceed them.

Sometimes my job can be a very lonely one, even surrounded by scores of people on a shoot day. I know it is all too easy to take the soft option – to produce a safe, average drive that folk are generally happy with – but I want more from a Castle Hill day than that. Sometimes this means I have to make a big call as Head Keeper and live with the consequences. I have to back myself, my judgement and my experience, even if this goes against what others might be thinking. So, yes, a shoot day can be and is very stressful. Also please bear in mind that I am running not just one such day over a season, but more than sixty. No wonder I am going grey!

Our loaders, in particular, also have to assess their clients quickly to ensure that they work well together. Each will have a different approach. For example, I know that Phil Lay always lets the gun make the first move in terms of conversation. Not all guns want to talk and some will be in a strong zone of concentration and just won't want to chat. Phil always focuses his attention on body language and this can be very important when a gun is not connecting with the birds. Knowing when to encourage and when to be quiet is perhaps the greatest art or gift. David Sexon is very good at correcting faults and encouraging success and I have, on occasions, moved David to help a gun who is particularly struggling.

At the other extreme is my old friend and rogue Peter Gould, who takes great delight in exchanging a lot of banter with the gun; he does have an amazing ability to strike up a relationship and cross barriers in a positive way with someone he has never met before. I know Peter will always establish early on where a gun has shot previously and his or her level of experience. Peter has also been known to have the odd wager with a gun about the cartridge-to-kill ratio he or she will have over the day. Peter, with thirty years' experience of loading, rarely loses such a bet!

If anyone thinks that being a loader is an easy job, they are sadly mistaken. Firing, and thus loading, 300 cartridges on a peg is not uncommon at Castle Hill. I take great pleasure when a loader, much to their own embarrassment, runs out of cartridges. This is, fortunately, very, very rare but when it has happened the loader concerned has accepted the fine of four bottles of port for the beaters' lodge with good grace. I know David Sexon got down to his last seven cartridges on a drive a few seasons ago and was getting pretty sweaty! A few years back, on the Smoldon's Bottom drive, I allowed the beat-keepers to beat the drive slowly, flushing birds in very small numbers over the team of guns. As a result the drive lasted twice as long as usual and ended with six out of the eight loaders running out of cartridges. The shoot was well supplied with port for several weeks as a result! My system of fines is usually restricted to the loaders and beat-keepers: those folk who are usually in my line of sight and have the greatest opportunities to commit a 'balls-up'. Peter Gould, with his annoying habits and wind-ups, usually receives a fine each time he attends a day for some misdemeanour or piece of cheek. Over the years I have known him he must have been fined hundreds and hundreds of bottles of port; he should have had shares in Taylor's!

Sometimes guns won't listen to or take advice from loaders, but this is rare, for usually the type of gun who comes to Castle Hill is here to really enjoy the day and the experience. For some this might simply mean that they connect with a bird that previously they could only have dreamed about hitting. For loaders such as David and Phil, loading is the next best thing to shooting. They share the enjoyment when their client is shooting well and hits that outstandingly high bird, as well as getting the buzz that comes from being part of a team. There is huge job satisfaction in helping a gun turn what might have been a mediocre day's performance into something better, or even great. As Phil has said to me, the guns that he loads for are real sportsmen or women who view Castle Hill as the premier league of shooting and for him to be able to help them achieve their goals, whilst witnessing the sport at its highest level, is a real privilege. Many of the loaders have developed a real partnership or friendship with the guns and I know that both David and Phil have had the honour of joining Prince Eric Sturdza when the Prince has shot in Spain and Argentina.

David and Phil came to be loaders at Castle Hill from two completely different directions. Wherever I have been keeper, I have always encouraged youngsters to get involved with the shoot, and more importantly to gain an understanding of the countryside. David joined the beating line at about the age of six, when I first arrived at Castle Hill. I think he spent most of his time lost, as his little legs meant that he could not keep up with the beating line! He was rightly teased by the then beat-keepers who would, on occasions, throw him over obstacles that he could not climb over. David would hang on to the five pounds per day he earned and over the season he would save a hundred pounds or more, which made him feel like a millionaire! David had caught the bug. From the age of seventeen he would join me some evenings as we tried to cull the odd fox and a year later I recruited him as a loader, with his first client being a gentleman named Tim Hoare, a stockbroker and a really good fun person. Tim is an easy-going, friendly guy and I knew the two would hit it off. It is really important to place loaders wherever possible with clients to whom they will relate well: choosing the right 'team' is vital.

I first met Phil in his role as a self-employed agricultural engineer, repairing farm machinery. I am a strong believer in using local businesses and employing local people where possible and Phil is one of these folk. The shooting season is a quiet time for him and many others whose primary income is linked to farming, so the money earned as a loader is a helpful way to supplement it. Although the money helps, I also know that Phil has the bug and loads for the simple enjoyment of seeing and appreciating top quality shooting. I first phoned Phil about five years ago to ask if he could help me out on a particular day. I was a bit mean to him on that first day as I put him double-gunning for a left-handed gun, which could not have been a more difficult baptism. Yet he survived, and even thrived, and is now one of our most reliable –

and cheeky – loaders.

Someone else who has to take a great interest in the guns and accurately assess all their requirements is Peter Baxendale. For the last eighteen or nineteen years he has been helping with the so called 'House Days' at Castle Hill, when a team of guns will shoot back-to-back days whilst staying in the Main House. Over the years these days have grown in popularity and a single House Day event in a season grew to three or four. Now, in 2014, we have around eight such bookings each season. These House Days are usually highly enjoyable, but often challenging. Although we frequently have repeat bookings, so I know what to expect, we also have some teams shooting with us for the first time and it is then that assessment and communication are even more important than usual.

Unfortunately I have been known, in my true 'bull-in-a-china-shop' fashion, to have sped off at the start of the day without a proper consultation with Peter, for which quite rightly I have later had to shoulder the blame. On one occasion, around three or four seasons ago, Peter brought a team of Americans to Castle Hill. I am afraid that I left the House without telling Peter where we were going for the first drive. I later discovered that the team were somewhat nervous and needed to be reassured of their shooting abilities at the beginning of the day. I, however, knew that the weather conditions meant that Brayley would shoot well as a first drive. Indeed it did, and the team fired over 1,000 cartridges, but, regrettably, for a total of only ninety birds. Peter informed me that without thinking I had managed to traumatise the guns and I had to spend the rest of the day restoring their confidence.

On another occasion Peter brought a team of guns from North London. All were driving Range Rovers, none of which, I subsequently discovered, were fitted with suitable off-road tyres. Again in my haste I failed to realise this and took the guns to Kerscott for the first drive. The journey involved some serious 'off-roading'. As usual, I was in the lead vehicle, my Land Rover Defender, and

I could see in my rear-view mirror the carnage behind me as the Range Rovers slid and struggled over the terrain. The problem was further compounded when we found that the track ahead was blocked by a fallen larch sapling. Peter volunteered to remove it from the 'road', but before he could get out of his vehicle I told him not to worry and drove straight over it. The other cars followed and at elevenses there was some grumbling as to the effect of the larch on the vehicles' tyres. I was firmly put in my place when I was not offered a glass of champagne by the rather disgruntled guns. A lesson in observation and communication learnt!

Gamekeeping is perhaps associated in many people's minds with the control of poaching. I first came across the practice when working as a young keeper at Sherborne. I stumbled across a group of poachers running lurchers over a fifty-acre field in the early hours of a very dark morning. Perhaps rather fortunately, these guys were much fitter than I was and I could not catch up with them – for I can well imagine what this group of men might have done to me if they had decided to make a stand. Again in Dorset, this time when I was at Mapperton, I witnessed folk on various occasions shooting pheasants from the side of the road. I managed to pursue one gentleman in what was then my shoot vehicle, a canvas-topped Land Rover. However, his Mini was faster, and I lost him, but I was so annoyed by the man's cheek that I resolved to report the incident at the local police station. As I stood at the front desk, with the desk sergeant taking down the details, I looked up to see the offending vehicle pull up right opposite. The sergeant and I dashed over to the car just as the man was getting out of it, apparently off to visit his mother. The dead pheasant was found in the back of his car and we actually managed to obtain a prosecution for poaching on this occasion.

We were less successful at Castle Hill one night when I was phoned and told that flashlights had been seen near the mill, close to the river. I rang the neighbouring keeper at Temple, Mark Atkinson, and he and I, plus our beat-keepers, rushed as quickly as we could to the site. I think we all assumed that the lights came from deer poachers, but when we arrived there was no one to be seen. After thirty minutes or so of fruitless searching we were standing around chatting quietly in a gateway when Mark suddenly said, 'What's that chattering noise?' I could not hear anything at first, but then the noise came again and we realised it was coming from the nearby ditch. We both flashed our torches down and found two guys in wet suits huddled together trying to keep warm, but their chattering teeth had given them away! It was clear that the poachers were after salmon, but they had none on their person and both claimed that they were out 'picking mushrooms'. Without physical proof there was no chance of a prosecution but at least we had the satisfaction of knowing that the two had certainly suffered for their unsuccessful night's work. Their exploits were never repeated.

On arrival at Castle Hill I had been warned by a few of the locals about three or more guys who were renowned for their big-time deer poaching, and also that their methods could be quite unsavoury, with the use of dogs as well as rifles. Duly warned, I resolved to take a different method to that of apprehending them, for I certainly did not want to end up with some potentially unpleasant near-neighbours. I thus approached these guys directly and asked them to help me control the foxes on the Estate: I soon had them out lamping with me in teams of four. I also arranged for them to undertake various small tasks around the shoot and I now class them as friends, who no longer poach deer. Included in this group is Danny Yeo, who over the past fifteen years has become a reliable and dependable friend and helper with whom I regularly share a pint or two in our local pub. Danny now undertakes numerous tasks on the shoot, centred mainly on felling or cutting back trees, which he does with a great sense of humour, and he never presents me with a bill. He is a top guy. Whilst there are still a couple of well-known poachers in the area, the police are aware of them too, so my job is made easier.

CHAPTER SIX

'Prevention Better Than Cure…'

My job is complicated, but in a good way, by the fact that I am employed by the syndicate but work with and alongside the Estate. Naturally, many of the clients Peter Baxendale brings to Castle Hill are enthralled not just by the shooting and the stunningly beautiful Devon countryside but also by the House, its gardens and setting, as well as the accommodation and the entertaining opportunities that it provides. The shoot, including the one at Temple, and the House are now synonymous with the Estate and I know Lady Arran takes great pride in that it all works so well together. The Fortescue family has always shown a keen interest in shooting. Lady Margaret Fortescue very much enjoyed joining the picking-up team when she was able and sometimes came out twice a week. Lady Arran has the responsibility of making sure everything in the House is perfect for the guns on their return and will often join them for lunch in the shoot lodge. I am sure that she views both the Temple and Castle Hill shoots as real assets to the Estate and takes what might be termed a maternalistic approach to them and to their role in enhancing the name and reputation of Castle Hill around the world. From 2nd February to early October my job can be a lonely one but I always know that if I need to discuss something or offload about any issue I can roar into the courtyard by the Estate Office and find someone with whom to share a chat and a cup of tea, which is a great help and comfort.

Hugh Thomas moved on from the estate management side of Castle Hill around fifteen years ago, although he still deals with many of the legal requirements of the syndicate. Since Hugh's departure, Paul Smalley of Savills has handled the estate and business management at Castle Hill. He deals with the let property and its maintenance directly with the tenants, as well as overseeing repairs to the main buildings and all Estate activities overseas. His involvement with forestry management means that he is the first port of call for both shoots and it is in this area that I have most contact with him. We speak quite regularly, though usually at speed! As is my way, I announce my arrival by tearing into the yard, shout a loud greeting to Margaret on reception, grab a quick chat with Paul – usually in my role as eyes and ears for the Estate, for frequently it is I or my keepers who first spot a fence down or a fallen tree blocking a route – and then I roar off again. The meeting is usually over within five minutes!

Although I like to think that I do have a good overall view of the Estate and how its many components interlock or overlap, I am first and foremost the Head Keeper. Historically the opposing demands of forestry and game birds can be an area of conflict, if not a battleground. Certainly it is on this subject that Paul and I have our greatest discussions. We both try our best to resolve areas of disagreement but sometimes each of us will dig our heels in. That said, our relationship is not one of confrontation but of compromise, and if either of us feels really strongly that something is the right thing to do we will compromise elsewhere.

The forestry on the Estate is mainly soft wood with about twenty per cent of it larch. When soft wood is at the end of its growing life it needs to be felled, for as trees start to die they will fall over. Of course this can be dangerous and also represent a financial loss in terms of the wood, so I do understand that on occasions trees need to come down. However, with my gamekeeper's hat on, the felling of trees can alter a drive completely. At its worst, tree-felling can turn a fantastic drive into nothing in the space of one season. Naturally I am loath to see this happen but I can understand that sometimes the removal of trees is part of the bigger picture for the Estate. Paul has known me long enough to realise that if I am really digging my heels in, then it must be vital for the shoot and a really good reason for my intransigent position.

A good example of us working together concerned the larch trees on the Eggesford Bank drive, all of which had come to the end of their natural cycle and were ready for felling. I was none too keen on this happening so Paul and I came up with a plan whereby two-thirds were felled, leaving behind those that I believed to be the most important trees for the drive to stand a little longer. Equally, however, changes in forestry occur naturally. Trees grow and birds that were once easily visible on a drive become obscured. Trees die or are felled and alter the very nature and success of a drive. All such changes can occur either dramatically, say as the result of a storm, or very slowly with the growth of trees, but a good keeper reacts quickly to these changes and where possible plans for them.

Unfortunately, larch trees across Europe have been affected by *phytophthora ramorum*, a fungus-like plant pathogen that causes extensive damage and mortality. The disease is fairly relentless and the Estate has not escaped its ravages. The first attack was in 2011 and then in July 2013, just after the birds had arrived, we discovered the disease in some of the larch trees within one of the pens. Naturally, we had only just moved the pen into this location, having found that the previous site was too damp for the birds! As is the norm, we received a felling order from the Forestry Commission to fell the larch by the autumn. This presented us with a bit of a dilemma but together Paul and I made the decision to fell the affected trees as soon as possible, so as to minimise any disruption during the actual shooting season. Hence the young pheasants were herded to one end of the pen to keep them away from the felling contractors, who luckily worked speedily. Paul agreed to my request that the mess of small branches, twigs, the 'lop and top' and so on, could be left in the pen to give extra ground cover. At some point, arrangements would have to be made to go back and remove this debris, which would be more costly for the Estate than removing it at the time of felling, but Paul could see my point of view. There was a great deal of sense in keeping the cover there for the season. Dealing with the infected larch trees as we did was a classic compromise on both our parts.

Regrettably, the adjacent compartments of larch have also had to come down, as they too became infected with this dreadful disease. Its relentless nature means that it is highly likely to decimate all the larch within the next few years. Of course, it is the responsibility of both Paul and me to manage this process as well as we can. We have agreed that 'panic' felling should be avoided, both on economic grounds and in terms of too sudden and dramatic an alteration to the skyline of some of the drives. Also there is a chance, however slim, that the Estate might just escape the worst of the spread of the disease.

We cannot predict how the necessary felling might adversely affect the shoot, but I take some comfort from the fact that although the remaining third of the larches on the Eggesford Bank drive have now themselves succumbed to *phytophthora* and have had to go, we are still able to shoot the drive and it seems to be working reasonably well, if not quite as well as it was. What is clear is that from the shoot's point of view I will have to be creative in my response to both the risk and the effects of the disease. In addition both Paul and I must try to anticipate future problems and liaise closely on the replanting programme.

One idea being seriously considered is for the Estate to have more hard wood planted than soft; in terms of a thirty-year legacy, hard-wood planting should result in some fantastic woodland for shooting. Hard woods have the advantage over soft in that they can be more easily managed, thinned and cropped without having to remove all the cover, but they do cost more to plant and have a longer 'harvest' time. Whilst soft woods will take fifteen to twenty years to reach a decent height, it can take twice as long as that for hard woods to reach the same dimensions. With Paul's approval we are planting berry-producing trees, such as beech and sycamore, which will eventually be harvested mainly for firewood, but during their lifetimes will also be a great food source for our wild bird population. In addition, as such trees grow, they create a useful forest floor cover of brambles and other wild plants, which a soft-wood forest does not allow due to the fact that light is restricted. Of course, the economics of the Estate dictate that soft woods will still continue to be grown alongside the other species – traditionally Castle Hill has specialised in high quality Douglas fir.

Although shooting is currently the Estate's most important tenant, along with Velcourt, the main dairy farming tenant, who can predict whether this will be the case in thirty years' time? Decisions made now as to planting for shooting are being made in good faith but no one knows what the world of shooting will be in the future. Hopefully the work we are doing now will mean that Castle Hill will still be at its pinnacle, but shooting may alter dramatically and the work we are doing now may be superfluous. If the legacy of shooting means that in thirty years' time the Estate has more hard wood than soft, would that be a disaster? There will always be a market for firewood, especially with the rate at which wood burners seem to be being installed, so I don't think either Paul or I lie awake at night worrying about the implications for the future of the replanting decisions we make now.

Another of the tasks of any gamekeeper is that of pest control. I have an important role in trying to reduce the grey squirrel population on the Estate. Not only are these furry pests a nuisance when they attack my feeders, they are of course a real problem on the Estate for, with all the food available, it is like a 'Harrods Food Hall' for rodents. They can do extensive damage to the forestry stock and both Paul and I exhibit perhaps a rather obsessive, but understandable, interest in their control.

We have tried all sorts of devices and systems to keep the squirrel population down and our latest attempts have utilised a gas-powered trap. This piece of kit has an opening baited with peanut butter which the squirrel explores head first. As soon as movement is detected a metal bolt is fired, which enters the animal's head, dispatching it quickly and humanely without suffering. Unfortunately this machine has proved itself to be unsuccessful at controlling its intended prey but has claimed two human victims. One day I attached the trap to a tree and a few days later noticed that it had not been 'fired'. I stopped my Land Rover, got out and went to see if it was functioning properly. I did so by putting my fingers into the bait-hole and duly had the nasty surprise of the bolt firing into my hand! I removed the whole trap and took it to Paul's office to show him. Seeing my bloody hand, Paul just about managed to hide his laughter. He took the trap from me, tried to demonstrate how it should be used, and he too ended up with the bolt in his hand! Squirrels 2, Pest Controllers 0.

On a serious note, our other traps, and the occasional shotgun, claim around 700 to 800 grey squirrels a year across the Estate. Such numbers demonstrate what a problem the country has as a whole with this particular species of vermin. Those animals that we kill go into a deep freeze and a local falconer collects them from us, so at least the meat does have some use.

The planting of cover crops has been at the heart of the success of the vast majority of the drives at Castle Hill. Much of what I learnt, often through trial and error, at Miltons and elsewhere on Exmoor has been applied to Castle Hill and, once again, I am still learning, adapting and adopting new crops to suit the topography, prevailing winds and soil types. We now have slightly over three hundred acres under cover crops in any one season on the Estate ground and adjoining land, and it is no secret that I would like more! This is one area in which I have had mixed success in dealing with Paul and the requirements of the Estate. He has been very helpful in negotiating over cover crops on tenanted farms when I want to add a drive, and recently we were able to add an east wind drive with the placing of suitable cover. Although the prevailing wind at Castle Hill is a south-westerly one, there are some days when the wind shifts easterly or north-easterly, and I was aware that the shoot was short of east wind drives. With Paul's help I identified and secured cover-crop ground to create what I wanted. The Estate has also helped the shoot by minimising the planting of maize in recent years, which has reduced the opportunities for birds to wander. Maize does act as something of a magnet for pheasants, given that they love the security, warmth and food that this crop provides. Even before this reduction in the planted acreage, and again in consideration of the shoot, the Estate had grown early maturing maize varieties so that they were harvested in September, before the birds could go 'walkabout' too much and before the start of the season.

It has now become something of a ritual each year for me to ask Lady Arran and Paul for a cover crop at a location named Oxford Down, and each year my request is turned down. To be totally fair, the Estate, both House and Gardens, are Grade I Listed, with all the restrictions that this implies to redevelopment and alterations. So sites like Oxford Down with its pinnacle hill, to me an ideal location for a cover crop, simply cannot be ploughed up. English Heritage has always taken a keen interest in the Estate and both Paul and Lady Arran are very aware of the need to work in harmony with this organisation. Landscape aesthetics may not be my number one priority but they are of great importance to the Estate and of course I respect and understand this. It is another example of the need for me to see the bigger picture; but this certainly does not stop me from being cheeky and trying to get away with the odd trick!

We have more than thirty drives at Castle Hill, all of which are fed to some extent by cover crops. For example on the Sandy Park drive (see diagram A), the guns are placed at the bottom of a very deep valley that initially slopes gently. We would normally only do this drive on a north-easterly wind as a back-up to the Kite's Nest drive on the other side of the valley, which is the westerly wind drive. Alternatively, we might do this drive as a 'catch-out' drive as the birds might have strayed away from Kite's Nest into Sandy Park. The cover crop is five acres in size with miscanthus grass in the centre of it. These grasses used to be surrounded by maize, but, due to the elevation of the drive and the nature of the soil, maize was a crop that struggled to thrive.

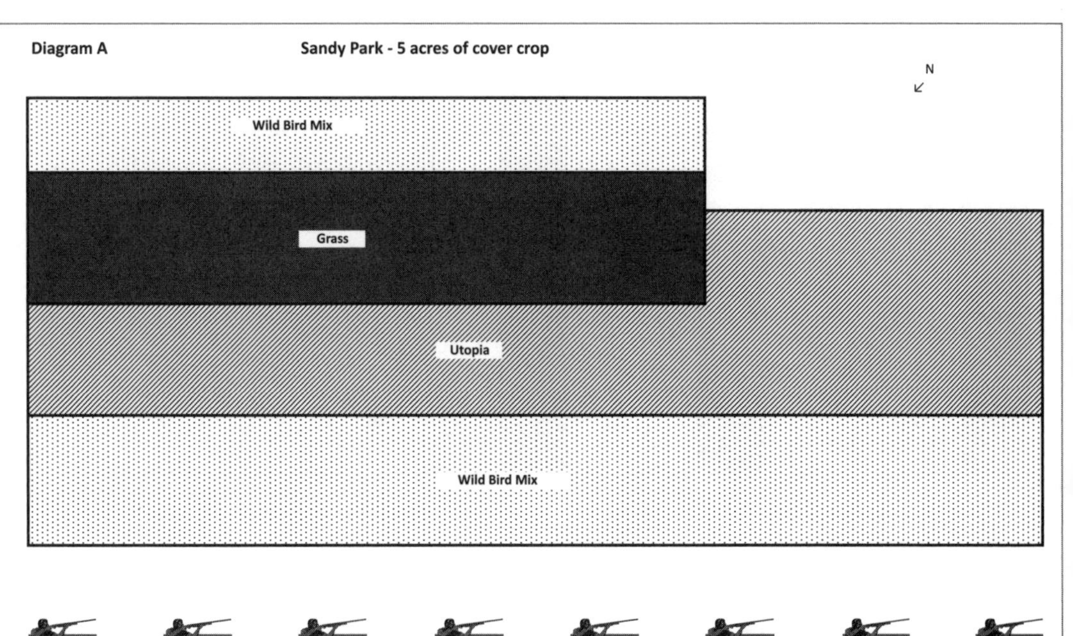

We also discovered that when the maize did grow well it would attract too many birds to this secondary drive, which is only half a field off our boundary, and we did not want to risk sending too many birds to that area and potentially lose them from our ground. After various discussions with seed companies it was decided to use Utopia instead, a hardy kale/mustard seed mix, that provides dense cover and grows three to four feet high to provide excellent warmth and security for the birds.

By contrast, Mays Quarry drive (see diagram B) is more of a traditional south-westerly wind drive, for in a north or easterly wind the birds will simply not fly high enough. Such winds seem to force the birds down and this is especially true if the wind is a cool one. I have learnt over the years that birds will not fly into a cold wind. The ten-acre cover crop for this drive includes a tree plot comprised of mainly Douglas fir, a few laurels and the odd hard wood tree. I planted the firs and laurels in my first or second year at Castle Hill. At the very front of the plot are scrubby trees

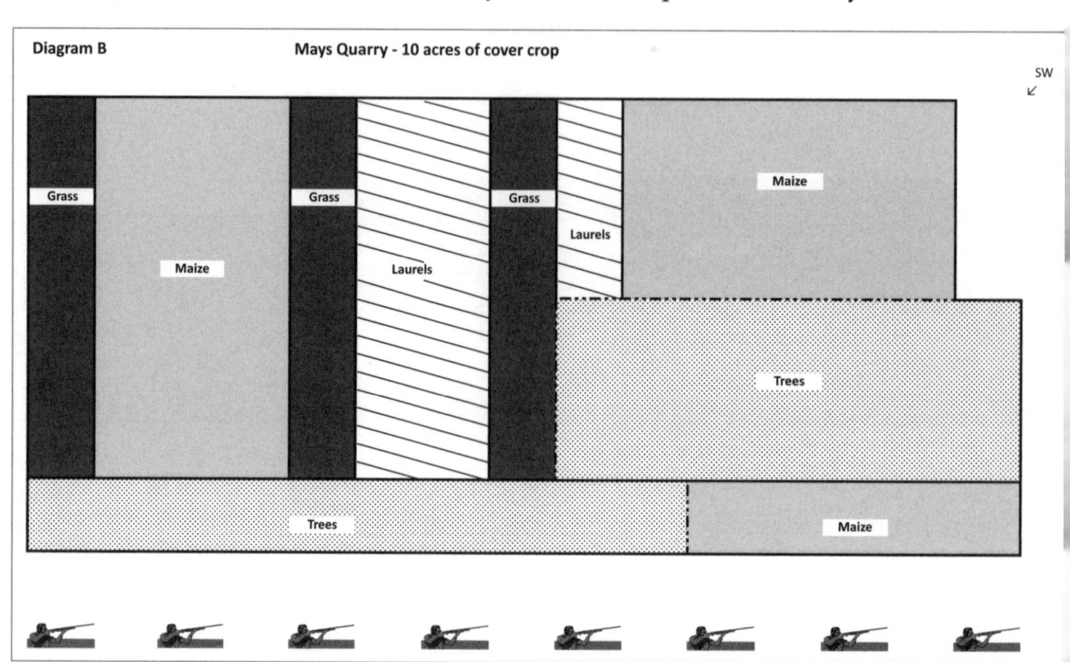

and bushes planted by the previous keeper, which have reached a height of twenty feet at their maximum.

The maize grown at the back of the drive, behind the trees, is to give extra height to the birds: they rise and then have to rise again to get over the trees. The belts of laurel stop the wind coming in and make it nice and warm for the birds, whilst the maize draws them in and keeps them. The miscanthus grasses are planted in five-metre strips or belts, which help to protect the maize. Miscanthus grows earlier than maize and provides a barrier for it from both wind and rabbits, encouraging healthy maize growth. At the same time, the grasses also reduce soil erosion and provide some support for the mature maize as well, meaning that this crop is less likely to get blown over early in the season.

One thing I would like to stress is that we never depend solely on maize as a cover crop, good though it is. The climate in the West Country is such that we cannot rely on it to grow and flourish each year and, to mix a metaphor, putting all our eggs in one basket would be folly. Like any business, we spread the risk and plant other cover crops too. In addition, the strips of miscanthus, or whatever crop it may be, allows the birds to move from a plot of maize into somewhere else; it gives them an escape route so that the drive is not over in one massive flush of birds. The same huge flush would occur on the Brayley drive if it was not for the presence of mature laurel trees, some now twenty-five feet or more tall, which provide the birds with the opportunity to slip out of the maize. We are then able to push the birds steadily over the guns from the patch of laurels. Maize also tends to deteriorate over the season; up until the end of November the crop may be fully upright, allowing us to flush the birds in a controlled way, but later in the season it thins and falls and birds will too readily flush from it – so the back-up of another strip of cover for the birds to utilise is vital.

Whilst I am still a fan of maize as a cover crop we have, as I say, been forced with the recent poor summers to recognise its limitations. Pheasants just love the easy availability of food within a maize crop and rarely wander far from it. In addition, the spaces between the rows allow the birds to fly well out of maize. Unfortunately, it is a greedy crop, and after a few years of planting it does exhaust the soil. In wet years maize is also susceptible to a disease called 'eye-spot' on the leaves, when small, black spots appear. Once this is established the crop soon withers and dies and will certainly not last the season. For this reason, along with our constant search for improvement, we have been forced to look at alternatives. Miscanthus has now become an established cover crop at Castle Hill and it works well. In addition, this past year (2013) we planted over 10,000 laurel bushes. Not only do these provide shelter and warmth for the birds, but once laurel has taken root, it is fast-growing, hardy and is around for years.

For the past few seasons we have been trialling the use of a wild bird mix as a cover crop; it is composed of such goodies as buckwheat, linseed, barley and mustard. This is very attractive to the birds and draws them in, particularly early in the season. Pheasants soon learn that there is food available elsewhere as well as in the pens and we have found that this type of cover crop at least entices them to where we want them to be.

The Mays Quarry drive is beaten in a sort of three-tier, pincer movement. If we lined up the beaters at the back of the drive and simply beat straight down, then the birds would flush in all directions with just a few going over the guns. This drive is one that we beat more than others; depending on the wind direction it may be beaten ten, twenty or even thirty times in a season. As I stand behind the gun line, I can see the first birds flushing; despite the many times I have seen this drive beaten, no one day is the same. This is when the radio becomes essential so that I can control what is happening in front of me, up in the cover crop. The beaters on one side might need to move further on than the other, or the back line might need to come forward slightly quicker, or even briefly stay still; all is so dependent on the exact direction of the wind, its speed and the atmospheric conditions. Of course the ultimate aim, as ever, is to send high, challenging birds over the gun line in steady, controlled numbers, and to provide shooting for all eight guns. Thus the beating line has to be constantly adjusted: for example, if the birds are being pushed towards, say, the back and the left-side beaters, I will instruct these two lines to move on more quickly, which will alter the spread of the birds along the gun line.

Generally, on any drive, we do try to launch the birds well before the end of the cover crop is reached, so that they are forced to go even higher over the trees before reaching the guns. I have found that if birds are driven up just before a wood they tend to go straight up and are then descending towards the guns rather than still rising. This of course is far from ideal and will probably result in a general massacre of my birds. Having said that, there is no hard and fast rule and each drive will have its best 'launch pad', so to speak, from which the birds will take off and become strong fliers, and go over the line in an even spread. Finding this spot can only come with experience, but if we can shepherd the birds in such a way that they take off from or at least near it, then the rest of the drive becomes much less of a worry.

I have a diagram of each drive, with the various cover crops outlined, and before each season I will sit down with the beat-keepers to look at each one, for crops will change, not just in variety, but also in acreage. Each drive will be discussed individually, and in detail, so that when we come to beat them, whether for the first time or for the twentieth that season, all will know their tasks and responsibilities. I never want either myself or the beat-keepers to fall into the trap of thinking that just because we have beaten a drive for so many years in a particular way, it will work out just fine by doing what we have always done. Such thinking is pure complacency and is bound to result in failure at some point.

I am so proud of all those good folk who come out to help on a shoot day. The beat-keepers do a wonderful job in what are sometimes difficult circumstances and our pickers-up and loaders are all very professional. Perhaps the most unsung heroes on a shoot day are those in the beating team, most of whom are uncomplaining as I ask them to beat yet another drive at the end of a hard day. They have to put up with my constant demands and occasionally my temper but their sense of camaraderie and fun sees them through the day. We have one particularly talented beater, Gillian Tredgold, who has a love of poetry and of writing mischievous tales: she has written many words about events that have happened on shoot days. Gillian's sense of fun, and that of her fellow beaters, was described perfectly in her 'Rules For Beaters', written a few years ago, which, I think, sum up the average day for beaters at Castle Hill. There is also just the tiniest dig at me!

RULES FOR BEATERS

Brian says please note that this year the maize is rather tall; therefore, beaters have several options:

a) Leave a trail of breadcrumbs when walking through maize – easier to find your way back when you follow them!

b) Tie a piece of string to the first maize stalk as you enter, and carry it through to the end. This way you can find your way back!

c) Beaters all join hands and walk down one track together, therefore all stay in contact and nobody gets lost!

d) When walking through maize, watch out for anything coming the other way, i.e. stags, badgers or any lost beaters left over from last season.

e) Whistle or sing loudly all the way through so somebody knows you are there. If Head Keeper yells at you to shut up, just tell him to p*** off!

f) Better still, refuse point blank to go into the flippin' maize in the first place!

Along with the placement and choice of cover crops, another crucial factor is the location of release pens. I believe three elements need to be considered here: open air, ground cover and the opportunity for the birds to roost and feel secure doing so. Regarding ground cover within the pens, it is not always possible to find a site with sufficient cover, such as ferns and brambles, so we are frequently forced to plough up the ground within them (which, as you can imagine, can be difficult to do), and we plant mustard. Not only does this crop provide good ground cover, but it grows rapidly and early and is thus well established by the time we release the birds into the pens in late June and early July. Also, when it flowers, the plant attracts a great many insects that provide an added 'natural' food source for the birds at a crucial time in their development. This insect life also has the advantage of reducing pecking and bullying amongst the birds, which can be prevalent when they are bored. The insects focus the birds' attention away from fighting, so not only provide extra nutrition but reduce damage and stress amongst the pheasants. In addition, substantial areas of mustard within the pens, up to five acres, allow the birds to spread out and explore, rather than bunching together: this reduces the risk of disease and soil contamination from fouling. The use of mustard is an added cost to the shoot, but in my view it easily pays for itself in terms of less damage to the birds, reduced disease, and fewer birds lost to raptors.

When locating and building a pen I always try to include an element of woodland, for it is important to provide a secure roosting area for the birds at night. As the birds develop and move away from the release pen, they will not return at night if they do not feel secure and this could result in the loss and straying of birds. On the other hand, I would never position a pen solely under trees or in a woodland setting for too many trees will reduce the flow of air through the pen, which is so vital in terms of disease prevention. We also avoid areas of stagnant water near feeding areas at all costs, for the birds will foul the water and then drink it, meaning that disease will soon become an issue. If the ground is not free-draining we will put stone down to level such areas and thus avoid water collecting in puddles. We are also careful as to where we go in the pen to feed the birds, for continuous use of the same tracks will create ruts for water to find. Rather than using the same paths year after year, we create fresh 'highways' each year and endeavour to flatten and firm-up the ground so as to reduce the risk of puddles forming.

Ideally, once the three critical elements are satisfied, I will usually try to locate a pen on the opposite side of the valley to where the guns will be placed, so that when the birds are flushed from a cover crop their flight-line means that they are heading back towards the pen. Our pens are large in comparison with many shoots. For example, the release pen for the Deer Park drive is twenty-six acres in size, whilst Kite's Nest is served by a thirty-acre pen. In other locations one pen might be feeding birds into three or four drives.

There is much ill-informed criticism of the density of bird numbers on large shoots such as Castle Hill and those on Exmoor. High density is viewed as increasing the risk of disease and causing unnecessary stress to the birds. Whilst there is no doubt an element of good or best practice in this argument, I firmly believe that the issue can be addressed by looking at the environment in which the birds are placed. We place around 8,000 birds in the twenty-six acres of the Deer Park release pen, which may seem like a large number, but we have worked very hard to produce a habitat that supplies both security and diversity – trees, mixed ground cover and hedgerows – and the birds thrive there.

Yet during last season (2012-13) I began to worry that our release pens were possibly slightly too small for the number of birds. Whilst we had no disease issues, I felt we should consider enlarging our two main pens and this we have done, so that we now have 320 acres set aside for the release pens, requiring a huge amount of maintenance. All the pens are sited on good, draining soil, with plenty of shade and water, and I think are a credit to the hard work of the five gamekeepers who work on the Estate. We have spent a great deal of time and effort in trying to improve the pen environment for the birds. For example, and again always trying to reduce the levels of stress for the birds, we have looked at trying to minimise the opportunities for birds of prey to find a suitable perch near a pen, by cutting back branches or even felling trees. We have tried to provide sunny areas in the pens so that the birds can warm themselves or dry out after rain and we have also looked at ways of providing shade and cover. This has been 'trial and error' over a ten-year period, but I think the reduction in sickness amongst our birds is testament to the fact that we have been doing some things right!

I firmly believe that pheasants should be reared with as little chemical and medical intervention as possible. I am convinced that as close to organic as possible is the way it should be and I am particularly proud of our achievements at Castle Hill in this regard. I suppose it is in the area of disease prevention and the welfare of the birds that I most have to 'think like a pheasant'. I hope, certainly on Exmoor, that the days of either denying problems exist or simply throwing medication at the birds have ceased. Of course they need to be wormed and we take all necessary measures to prevent coccidiosis. I am delighted to say that during the season of 2012-13, one of the wettest, most miserable on record, we did not have to call out a vet once. The hard work we put into prevention rather than cure really pays off. I would actually argue that all the rain we have had in the past year or so has actually helped to flush out the ground in the release pens and, despite the mud, this has been of benefit. We have introduced some stone areas, not just around the feeders but elsewhere in the pens too, so as to give the birds places to escape the mud and we hope this will further enhance their strength and reduce the risk of disease.

Over the past fourteen or fifteen years I have developed a strong relationship with our vet, Alan Beynon of the St Davids practice outside Exeter, who is undoubtedly the foremost game-bird vet in the country. Both Alan and I are of the same mind, in that we would always rather prevent problems than cure them. Alan spends a great deal of his time travelling up and down the country to visit shoots and advise on disease prevention. The game side of the practice has grown so much that five vets are now employed solely in this field and operate throughout the UK. Alan began his career as a specialist poultry vet but was approached a number of years ago by a couple of game-rearers who had issues with their birds, with the proviso that everything was kept very confidential.

Alan would admit that the skills and knowledge he now possesses have been gained from a self-taught process, enhanced by a healthy dose of practical experience from keepers such as myself. Rather depressingly, in the early days much of Alan's work concerned post-mortems, in other words trying to find the cause of a problem after it had occurred, rather than the preventative approach that he favours today. That is not to say that post-mortems don't still feature in Alan's work, but now they are more likely to be on game-farm birds that are sacrificed to see if there are any underlying illnesses in the stock. If something is highlighted under a microscope, then action can be taken before the problem becomes business-threatening across the whole farm. In the early days, game-rearers would often bring their problems to Alan, but it wasn't long before he started to visit them at their premises so that he could observe the procedures and rearing conditions and enhance or alter them so as to prevent issues arising in the first place. Soon he extended this practice to include visiting shoots themselves and Exmoor was one of the first areas on Alan's list.

As news of his success with analysing game-rearing problems began to filter out, Alan received more and more discreet phone calls from gamekeepers. I suppose no one wants to admit to a problem and gamekeepers are perhaps more secretive than most. Alan has stories of 'cloak and dagger' meetings in pub car parks where he would be met by worried gamekeepers, who would then bundle him into the back of their vehicles to avoid prying eyes. In the competitive world of driven game shoots, the suspicion that a shoot has sickness problems with its birds could result in the loss of both bookings and reputation, so this clandestine approach can perhaps be understood.

As I say, I got on really well with Alan from the first time I met him when I took some dead birds in to his practice for a post-mortem. He discovered that they had suffered from *hexamita meleagridis*, which is an intestinal parasite. I think Alan found my attitude either rather scary or inspirational – I am not sure which! For rather than taking the diagnosis at face value and accepting the medication offered, I was keen to have all the answers to all the questions I could think of – why, what, how. I wanted to gain an exact understanding of the causes of the illness and what prevention measures I could take to avoid the problem in the future. I learnt that hexamitiasis is a disease that has long been associated with a high density of birds and, although this can be an element, stress is the main factor that makes birds more susceptible to it. Alan explained that hexamitiasis is difficult to treat and that prevention is a far better option so together we looked at ways of reducing stress levels, such as making sure the poults had access to enough feeders and drinkers and that these were sited in the right places. Crucially, we also deduced that the first day or so when the poults are placed in the release pens is when their stress levels would be at their highest. The birds tend to scatter to seek out their perimeters and the majority will then bunch up against the fence line. Traditionally I, and I know many other keepers, site feeders and drinkers in those parts of the pen that allow us easy access, usually somewhere in the middle. Thus in those first few hours, until the birds have really explored their new environment, many would be unable to feed or drink. Some would die, but others would become very stressed, which would make them more susceptible to disease around ten days after they had first entered their new surroundings. Alan pointed out that if the birds had acquired a disease at the game farm it would have shown within a day or so, so he convinced me that my outbreak of hexamitiasis was caused by factors under my control. Naturally I wanted to do something about this.

Traditionally, a vet would complete a post-mortem on a bird, discover the problem and treat the others with drugs. The following season the drugs would be administered before the problem arose again. As you can see, I was unhappy with this approach and I found Alan to be very receptive to my way of thinking; I told him that I was keen to try to alter the environment in which the birds found themselves and to make it better for them so that they could flourish. I am convinced that birds do fall ill when they are stressed and that their environment has a direct influence on stress levels.

I have spent many decades looking at and watching pheasants and I think I have gained a real understanding of their behaviour and what makes them flourish and thrive and, conversely, I seem to know when things are not quite right in their world. The secret to strong, healthy birds is the correct environment: simple as that. It has become another obsession for me to try to create this perfect habitat for them, so I will always look at various factors when birds are ill to try to discover if there is anything in how they are fed, watered and reared that may have impacted upon their health. I will also look at the same when the pheasants are not sick, to try to work out what we are doing right. I then have the luxury of being able to share my observations with Alan and we work together to see if my theories might be correct. If we think they are, then I can share them with others.

One disease that we have not suffered from at Castle Hill is mycoplasmosis, or 'bulgy eye'. Alan and I are convinced that this is due to the policy operated on the Estate of removing birds from the shoot at the end of the season. I would like to emphasise that this is a common practice across Exmoor shoots and we have all, touch wood, been spared the horrors of this disease. Both hens and cocks are caught, with the hens being sent to small nearby shoots and game farms for breeding stock. We thus give the ground time to recover before the new poults arrive four months later and also any disease organisms lurking in the soil will die away. The practice is the industry standard for poultry farms to ensure that disease is kept to a minimum and it seems to have worked on Exmoor too.

Periodically we have suffered, like all shoots, with problems from worms. I have reacted in two ways. I do use worming agents in the food, perhaps more liberally than some shoots, and of course there is a cost to this approach. However, I do take a different view from that of the industry standard to avoid worm problems. Traditionally, worming agents are applied when the poults first arrive: this is often when the weather is dry and the prevalence and breeding of worms are at their lowest. I prefer to worm when the wetter weather comes in and worm growth is at its highest, and then I continue to apply the wormer throughout the season. I have also looked at how and where we feed. As I have said, it is the norm for keepers to follow the same well-worn path through a pen to top up the feeders, and it is also fairly common practice to scatter pellets along paths and in areas where the birds congregate. The result is that the birds are walking over the same, potentially worm-infested areas all the time and this, combined with the densities such a feeding regime causes, means that illnesses from worms are more likely. Consequently every season we try to feed in different areas, moving the birds around the pen to fresher ground where worm-egg infestation is less likely. Although this policy has not eradicated the problem completely, we have seen a marked reduction in cases as a result.

Alan gave me the confidence to stick my head above the parapet and admit that Castle Hill, like many other shoots across the country, had its fair share of disease and sickness. At the time, such honesty was a bit revolutionary. However, I reasoned that unless the gamekeeping fraternity recognised and acknowledged its problems, it could not really expect to solve them, whether individually or as a group.

Because of Alan's connections with both rearers and gamekeepers, and the confidence they had (and have) in his integrity and skill, he was ideally placed to root out any problems. If poults were delivered aged six weeks and a few days later they appeared unwell, then the natural reaction was for the concerned gamekeeper to attribute the blame to the rearer. This could result in some rather lively exchanges, with Alan sometimes viewed as something of an arbitrator. Really, though, he was, and is, mostly concerned to find a remedy and try to prevent any recurrence. The usual pattern was for him to follow the progression of the birds from their early lives on the game farm through to their delivery to the shoot and then to study the crucial first couple of weeks in their new home. On occasion, Alan would discover that the disease or sickness issue rested firmly with the shoot: such news was not always well received.

Personally, I suppose my inquisitive and perfectionist nature meant that I always regarded Alan's findings as very helpful. Rather than ignore the problem or get into a game of blame and counter-blame, I preferred to use the results of his observations as an opportunity to discover what had gone wrong and try to prevent it happening again.

The measures he suggested did not always work and some were based on trial and error but because of our mutual respect, allied to my determination to grasp and eradicate sickness issues, Alan and I did manage to work very closely together. Through my chairmanship of the regional NGO (National Gamekeepers' Organisation) I was able to persuade most keepers, particularly those from Exmoor, to discuss bird welfare issues openly. I was not surprised to discover that the problems I was having were common to the majority. By openly sharing our experiences and the treatments we had tried, we could learn from each other and gradually form an universal 'good practice' guide when it came to disease prevention and cure. As I have said, Alan really helped us to move beyond the stigma of admitting to a problem: once that was achieved, we could combine our expertise as a region to offer solutions and suggestions to improve bird welfare nationally.

Two years ago, in 2012-13, despite, or because of, the terribly wet summer and autumn our birds managed to avoid any serious illness issues. In analysing why this was the case, Alan and I concluded that the rain had washed away bird droppings and thus removed a major disease-risk issue. Also, because of the wet state of the ground, we decided to release the birds from the pens earlier than we would have done in a normal summer. This reduced the bird densities, again removing a potential disease-risk factor, and although this meant that we had to spend extra hours ensuring that the birds did not stray from the shoot, we remained problem-free, with quality birds. Such thinking on your feet is so crucial but is so often overlooked. As a keeper, I firmly believe that you must always be assessing the health of your birds and must react accordingly – and this does not always mean a rush to the medicine cabinet.

I speak from long experience when I say that the approach I refer to as 'active observation' does mean that many hours can be spent just watching and learning about your birds. But any keeper who views his charges' welfare as of paramount importance has to put the hours in. This is undoubtedly when a keeper must think like a pheasant. To take an obvious example, if he or she notices that the birds do not react well to a wind from a certain direction, wind-breaks such as laurels should be planted in or near the pen to alleviate the problem in the future. When it comes to the welfare of the birds, a keeper must never stop thinking and assessing how best to improve their environment.

When we come to site a new pen, we don't just look at how that pen might feed certain drives or how the birds might be expected to fly over the gun line, but also keep firmly in our thoughts the pen itself and its environment and how best to design it to suit the birds. We will assess where the sun rises and sets, the availability of water, the prevailing wind, where the birds can roost, and so on. In my experience, if disease can be avoided by thinking about the birds' environment then other factors become almost superfluous, for strong, healthy birds will produce quality shooting for our guns. The traditional view of where to place a pen, i.e. to ensure the birds fly over the guns, becomes a secondary consideration. Because of the historic placement of pens at Castle Hill, many of which cannot readily be relocated without threatening the success of a long-standing main drive, our hands are tied to some extent. Both Alan and I have noticed that disease and sickness is marginally higher in these older pens, which just goes to show that the placement of all new pens should give the utmost consideration to pheasant welfare. We do tend to use more medicines in the older pens (again as a preventative measure) than we do in the newer ones.

We receive our poults at Castle Hill in June. Some people may regard this as something of a luxury, in that we are able to afford to take them several weeks earlier than most shoots. However, our focus is on high-end quality, as the good folk who shoot at Castle Hill expect the best. By receiving the birds earlier than some, we can guarantee that we have poults from the first hatch, which are generally stronger than later hatches. In addition, we are able to feed and rear them in accordance with the guidelines that have been proven to work over many years: we can keep a close eye on the young birds for signs of disease and react accordingly. It is at this time that we are most active in using preventative drugs, including worming agents in the feed as well as Avatec, which helps to prevent coccidiosis.

I haven't clipped the birds' wings for over ten years at Castle Hill, although a couple of beat-keepers still do. My birds are free to fly out of the pens as soon as they are able. I feel that the benefit of the birds exercising as early as possible, so as to build up their muscle strength, outweighs the risk of birds straying. They know where their food is and, as I have previously mentioned, we don't seem to lose too many birds to adjoining shoots. In addition, by clipping the wings I believe the birds lose a crucial amount of their feathers, those that wrap around the back and side of the bird, which provide vital waterproofing against the West Country weather. Without these feathers the risk of the bird catching a chill is much greater and to avoid clipping is part of my philosophy of keeping the birds as natural as possible. An intact bird is also much more likely to be able to flee from both raptors and foxes and this reduces our losses to such predators.

In recent years, poor weather has often meant that there has not been the natural food to encourage birds to wander. This was particularly true over the season 2012-13 and although we spent many hours 'dogging in', to keep the birds in the required places, we found that all our efforts were rather wasted as the boundaries were mainly clear of birds who had stayed firmly near the feeders. I would love to have the courage one season not to do any 'dogging in' at all, for I am convinced that it makes little difference to where the birds will be found. The truth is that I am not brave enough and my team and I will religiously walk the boundaries with our dogs for the foreseeable future.

Over the years I have been approached to offer advice on establishing or improving existing shoots, both nationally and internationally. With the worldwide client base of Castle Hill, I have begun to receive invitations to visit shoots owned or run by some of our distinguished guests. Count Riprand von Arco, for example, has shooting rights over 5,000 acres of land one hour outside Prague in the Czech Republic and I have been there on a number of occasions to offer my advice, most recently in March 2014. The Count employs an English keeper and is passionate about his shooting. Communist rule has meant that much of the ground has been divided into small parcels amongst local people, although the Count does still have control over a 3,000-acre central block in which the topography does allow the keeper to show what one might call 'Devon pheasants'. Mostly, my recommendations have been focused on the placement of drives and release pens, which have obviously been complicated by the land ownership issues; I have also suggested the felling of some areas of conifer woods to improve the flight lines of the birds. I hope that these suggestions have been helpful and that the shoot has been improved over time, particularly in terms of the height and quality of birds shown.

Another frequent visitor to Castle Hill is Baron Jean-Pierre Berghmans and I have travelled to his estate in the Ardennes region of Belgium. The Baron also employs an English keeper and I have been able to offer some advice on the best location of drives as well as the species of pheasant that should be reared there.

I have visited Morocco, too, to cast my eye over likely ground as well as America. I joined my old NGO colleague, David Clark, on a trip to St Louis to offer our advice regarding a walked-up pheasant and quail shoot. I must admit this was more of a holiday than a serious consultation, but it was a very enjoyable visit and I think David and I were able to offer something back to our generous hosts. I have also travelled more recently with Alan Beynon to such shoots as Buccleuch in Scotland to offer advice on the release-pen environment. I always get a great deal out of such visits myself and hope any comments I make are appreciated.

On these trips I often find myself waking up in the most elegant, sumptuous surroundings and I almost have to pinch myself to believe that I have come so far from those early days at Sherborne. However, before I can run away with my own self-importance, I make myself realise that I have a job to do and that for all my experience and knowledge I am only in the position I am because others, such as Ron Knight, had over the years taken time to share with me their own thoughts and opinions. Although I receive some compensation for my time on these foreign trips, I have always felt that the sport of shooting has given me such a rewarding and enjoyable career that I want to give something back. Consequently, if I have been approached for advice by national or local shoots, I have been happy to give it with no thought of payment. As anyone who enjoys shooting game birds will know, we are all part of a community with shared beliefs and I strongly believe that it is a privilege to share with others the limited knowledge and expertise I have been lucky enough to acquire over my career. Similarly, I frequently receive visitors at Castle Hill in the off-season to view our set-up and ask for advice on all sorts of things, from designing and siting drives to selecting cover crops, pheasant welfare and disease issues.

My love of partridge, with all the challenges that these special birds present, both in terms of keeping them alive during the early weeks, retention and getting them to fly in the right direction on a drive, led me back to Exmoor long after I had moved to Castle Hill. I was convinced that a largely partridge-only shoot could flourish on Exmoor, as long as the right ground became available. I shared these thoughts with the Castle Hill syndicate members, who were keen to finance such a shoot with the intention of taking a few days a season for themselves, with the rest let. I had had my eye on the ground at Challacombe for a number of years, but, as usual, there were problems surrounding the ownership of the land, and that of the adjoining ground, which took some time to resolve. There was an additional complication in that the then Master of the Exmoor Foxhounds, Captain Ronnie Wallace, feared that a shoot at Challacombe would displace the well-established fox hunting. The Captain, who was tragically killed in a car accident aged eighty-two in the winter of 2002, was a larger-than-life character who could be cantankerous and charming almost in the same breath. He was something of a 'Godfather' figure in the area and it certainly seemed that the local landowners referred almost all decisions to Ronnie to gain his blessing.

Well, the Captain's opposition to a shoot at Challacombe was firmly set but Hugh Thomas and I thought we might be able to change his mind if we invited him and Caspar MacDonald-Hall to a meeting between principals, to be held at Hugh's house. We tried to make the meeting as friendly and informal as possible but, despite the drink flowing freely, the Captain would not move. In desperation I – much to the astonishment I think of Mr MacDonald-Hall – made a solemn promise that I would not shoot any foxes on the land which was to belong to the Challacombe shoot unless I caught the animal actually inside one of the partridge pens. The Captain paused for a moment, clearly contemplating my offer, and I briefly hoped that my rash assurance might have finally turned the argument. However, we were all to be disappointed when the Captain finally uttered the words: 'I am fundamentally opposed.' Thus ended the meeting!

Of course, shooting has one huge advantage over hunting in that a shoot pays to use the land over which it shoots, with the income going directly to landowners and farmers for both rights and game plots. This fact, I believe, finally enabled us to obtain the shooting rights at Challacombe, although the Captain's opposition and influence meant that the whole process took ten long years. Once all the formalities had finally been sorted out, I was asked by the syndicate of guns at Castle Hill to devise the drives and place the plots for cover crops to create around twenty-five separate drives. Working alongside my old colleague from Bulland, John Brooks, was a joy, and between us we were able to introduce to the world of shooting the now famous – or infamous – drives of Pixie's Rocks and Niagara, to name but two. Both these drives produce partridge in excess of 130 feet high, which are truly stunning. It took no time at all before the world's best guns were heading towards Challacombe. Indeed, the 200-foot-plus sheer cliffs of Pixie's Rocks in particular have produced many superlative-filled descriptions and this drive alone has drawn guns to shoot there.

That is not to say that everything was easy in our first years. As we were designing Challacombe to be solely a partridge shoot, we of course needed large numbers of birds. In fact we were forced to go to four separate game-breeders to meet our needs, the last of which caused us some concern by continually postponing the delivery-date for the poults. When the birds did finally arrive it was immediately clear that they had some sort of respiratory disease, which rapidly spread to our healthy birds. Indeed on one night we lost several hundred birds. On the advice of vet Alan Beynon we replaced, at some expense, our feed, substituting instead one coated with an antibiotic; this saved the remaining birds right at the last moment. Even so, this disaster almost cost us our first season and instead of shooting anticipated bags of 300 birds a day we were down to 150- to 200-bird days. Rearing partridges is a much greater challenge than that presented by pheasants, for a partridge is far more susceptible to disease and cold and far more likely to die than a pheasant. Hence it is a much greater financial risk too. However, if you know what to look for, react quickly and have a first-class vet like Alan on board, then the rewards are high both in terms of shooting pleasure and profitability. Financially this first year was not great but we were still able to show some fantastic birds, which established our reputation – soon to be enhanced in subsequent years.

The syndicate kept the shooting rights for a decade and I directly supervised the shoot for the first three seasons. These years included the miserable year of 2001 when, due to the restrictions imposed upon Exmoor by the dreadful 'foot and mouth' disease outbreak, we were unable to shoot. Although the disease came near to Castle Hill, we were not directly affected, but had, of course, to take the necessary precautions. Challacombe, however, was right in the middle of many serious outbreaks: the terrible decision not to shoot at all for that season had to be reluctantly taken. The syndicate acted most honourably and the two keepers employed at Challacombe were found roles at Castle Hill on the same pay and were even given half of their expected tips for the season. Rents were still paid to local farmers as well as the costs of cover crops and the syndicate did as much as it could to ensure that the financial burden of the outbreak was alleviated.

Soon afterwards, though, the syndicate members decided to step away and the ground was not shot over for a couple of years, much to my and John's disappointment. I must say, though, that supervising Challacombe and running Castle Hill was demanding, both mentally and physically, for I was not getting any younger! Having said that I would have liked to have kept the best Challacombe drives going so as to combine them with early season days at Castle Hill.

Fortunately for those who love quality partridge-shooting, a gentleman named Angus Barnes, of the Loyton Shooting Group, took on the rights around four years ago and through the hard work and dedication of Angus and his team the Challacombe shoot goes from strength to strength. It is now viewed by many experts as one of the best shoots in the country. I am proud of my small contribution to the development of the Challacombe shoot, but I would also like to say that I am even more pleased that Angus has invested so heavily in shooting on Exmoor. Not only does the Loyton Shooting Group make a significant financial contribution to the area – for example, they employ over twenty full-time gamekeepers – they have really bought into shooting there and seem to have most certainly grasped the need to balance the pressures of commercial shooting with a respect for both the environment and for those who have the privilege to live on Exmoor. As well as the rights for Challacombe, Angus now runs Combe Sydenham, Haddeo Pixton and Stuckeridge, as well as shoots away from Exmoor. Angus understands the shooting traditions of Exmoor and I, for one, am confident that these shoots will go on to have even greater success.

Strangely, although I am lucky enough to see some of the

best shots in the world perform at Castle Hill and at other shoots across Exmoor, I am not much of a shot myself. I think this is for two reasons. Firstly, I don't shoot that often and, like most things in life, practice does make perfect. Secondly, I don't think I want to kill the birds enough: I am not totally focused. One thing I do know, from having watched many top-quality guns over the years, is that if you really want to kill a bird, often at the limits of both range and ability, you have to be one hundred per cent committed. On two days of the season the syndicate shoot insists that I join them in the line, which is both a great privilege and hugely enjoyable. As I have spent the previous few months being rude to the guns about their shooting, it is only fair that they have the opportunity to get even and they definitely return my 'compliments' with interest! I usually find on these days that by the last drive I can connect with the birds as I get into the swing of things. I suppose one of the issues with my mediocre shooting performance at Castle Hill is that I still view the birds as my birds and perhaps I just don't have the heart to kill them.

Alan Sexon reminded me recently of an incident when he and I were fortunate enough to be shooting at the Tawstock shoot near Newbridge some years ago: he recalled that after one of the drives I returned to the game cart laughing my head off and holding a large, leafy branch that I added to the 'bag', instead of the high pheasant I had been aiming at! I suppose that this illustrates that I don't take myself too seriously when it comes to my own shooting at least, and that on such days I am simply out to enjoy myself.

Castle Hill has a very jovial, informal, unstuffy atmosphere throughout the year, but especially on shoot days, and this is something Caspar and I have striven to maintain. The syndicate guns always say that the gamekeepers dress better than the guns and I think that is totally accurate and perhaps appropriate. The success of Castle Hill is, I think, almost as much due to the relaxed atmosphere on a shoot day, as to the quality of the birds.

It is certainly true though that success breeds success and as the reputation of Castle Hill has grown it has become easier to attract guns to our days.

In analysing why Castle Hill stands out, I think the hard work and dedication of all those involved with the shoot is a major factor, yet there are many other places where folk are equally committed. Similarly, there are many places where you can go to shoot pheasants that are as high, if not higher, than those seen at Castle Hill. What is unique about the shoot is its setting and its consistency: it produces the numbers and the quality of challenging birds day after day, and drive after drive. Lots of shoots have two or four or six great high-bird drives but Castle Hill has the ability to produce high-bird days four times a week, throughout the season, across a large number of drives. It also still delivers 500-bird days in the last week of January. Perhaps where Castle Hill really has the edge on some of these other high-bird shoots is that it offers a greater degree of elegance than some. The House and the grounds are simply stunning and I know that many of our visitors, particularly those from abroad, are totally entranced by the setting that the Estate provides. Castle Hill is a very special place and I am delighted, and very proud, to have been associated with it, and its success, for so long.

CHAPTER SEVEN

'Not Always the Most Popular Guy...'

I am a strong believer in change. Indeed, I can be almost evangelical about it and I am aware that on occasions I have even been known to preach! Sometimes this has been to the converted, but often I have had to face folk who are reluctant to consider change at any price, who are suspicious of me and what I have to say. I know that I am not always the most popular guy in the room.

Of course this has never stopped me from saying what I think, for change usually means that both I, and the business I am working in, are moving forward: as I have already said, if you are not moving forwards you are going backwards. I sincerely believe that accepting the *status quo* is not an option. Yet I find myself working in an industry (for though many consider game shooting a sport or a pastime, it is, fundamentally, an industry) that has been notoriously slow to accept change. 'We do it like that because that is how it has always been done' is a sentiment that has been heard so many times on so many shoot days up and down the country, and it is one that, as you can imagine, raises my blood pressure. That is not to say that I do not believe in tradition; I am the first to defend the rights and customs of the countryside. I just don't think that because something has been done in a particular way for years it means that it is necessarily the right way. Innovation is essential in any industry and shooting is no exception to this rule.

When I first moved to Miltons, only around five gamekeepers were employed full-time on Exmoor shoots. The emphasis then was very much on local shooting, with a tendency to look at quantity rather than quality. Instead of driving birds from the tops of valleys, it was frequently the case that birds were driven from varying heights off their sides, or even from the bottom of them. Of course ballistic knowledge then was such that the quality of cartridges was not nearly so good then as what we have today; also the guns were simply not used to shooting high birds as they were rarely encountered during an average day. Furthermore, the home-reared birds were often not strong enough to achieve the heights that we see today. As I have previously said, I did not move to Exmoor with some great masterplan in mind to produce high birds, but I did want to show challenging birds. It soon became apparent to Alan Milton, to those who represented Roxtons and to me that the wonderful topography of the area would lend itself to presenting such birds. We did initially come across quite a lot of opposition from a minority of folk (some of whom wrote for the shooting press) who claimed that trying to shoot such high birds was invariably cruel. In their view, many birds would be pricked by shot but not killed outright, and these birds would be left to die in pain, days or even weeks later – or so such folk claimed.

At Castle Hill, we insist that all guns use plastic rather than fibre wads in their cartridges, for we sincerely believe, and furthermore can scientifically prove, that the spread of shot from such cartridges is superior. Thus the killing power is enhanced. Indeed I would go further and state that to shoot at high game birds using fibre wads is cruel, for the pattern blows and the pellet penetration is significantly less than that from plastic ones. I might even say that the use of fibre wads on some high-bird shoots makes these shoots look superior, for it appears that the presented birds are 'beating' the guns, whereas in reality birds are being pricked but not dispatched by the use of fibre-wad cartridges. A plastic wad produces a superior shot pattern, with a more condensed spread and thus greater penetration, which is why it is much more likely to kill a bird outright.

A few years ago I travelled up to Birmingham to visit the Lovell Express offices. I was given the opportunity to compare the effects of plastic- and fibre-wad cartridges on the company's 'pattern plates', which clearly demonstrated the superiority of the plastic wad. It is not just me who holds such views and indeed I was delighted to read the following words of renowned gun, shooting instructor and journalist Mike Yardley in a recent edition of *The Field* magazine (December 2013):

> *'Plastic wads have a number of advantages [over fibre]... The frontal cap improves ballistic performance and protects the bore, the base skirt is a most efficient gas seal and the "legs" betwixt the two are compressible and create a shock absorber...'*

I can almost hear the shouts of those folk who advocate the use of fibre wads crying out in derision: here am I, a defender of the countryside, actually supporting a product that litters and pollutes that very countryside! I suppose my view could be seen as a contradiction: I might even be accused of hypocrisy. Yet it should be remembered that I am working on an Estate that attracts some of the best guns in the world and these clients expect not only to shoot the most challenging of game birds but also to be armed with the tools, i.e. the correct cartridges, for the task. I am aware that plastic wads take years to biodegrade and that some people claim that they pose a risk to livestock. In my experience this has never been an issue. I have witnessed many a sheep or a cow showing a passing interest in, or sniff at, a discarded plastic wad, but I have never, ever seen an animal eat one.

However, due to concerns like these we are always looking for alternatives. For example, working with Dan Reynolds of Roxtons, in the near future we are going to trial a wad composed of vegetable fat, which should disintegrate/dissolve when it is subjected to rain water. Only time will tell if this form of wad offers the same killing power as a plastic one. Manufacturers are also looking at other options and Gamebore have recently introduced the Power House Range of 12- and 20-bore cartridges with a wool wad. It would seem that such wads expand more than fibre ones do, thus creating a better seal in the bore of the barrel and reducing gas leakage. Gamebore claim that the consequence of this expansion is a more consistent performance, with better patterns and a reduction in recoil. The technical details look impressive and, of course, there are some clear environmental advantages, although the cost of these cartridges is currently high. I only hope that time and greater use will clearly demonstrate the killing power of these and other 'green' alternatives.

For many, the issues surrounding the use of different types of wad is not just about penetration and killing power. There are clear safety issues with fibre wads, which can flip in the barrel, something I have seen and experienced on more than one occasion. Conditions are naturally wet in North Devon and Exmoor and it does not take much for a cartridge to swell and distort.

I find it somewhat frustrating that the choice of wad has become something of an issue centred on high-bird game shooting, which of course means that the shoots of Exmoor and North Devon have been rather under the microscope on this subject. Yes, we do shoot high birds, and yes, we do have large daily bags:

but we also want guns to go away knowing that they have killed birds rather than wounded them. The specialist teams of guns who arrive on Exmoor come with the experience, the expertise and the equipment, both gun and cartridge, to kill high birds and the majority do use plastic wads. Yet this choice is not simply a high-bird issue, for it also concerns safety, reliability and cost. I do not see any immediate change in our use of plastic wads, but we are very much open to new ideas and technologies. I do wish the debate could be wider and that a sensible discussion can be had so that the right conclusion can be reached for the good of shooting as well as the wider environment.

I must admit I dislike as much as anyone seeing plastic wads littering the ground. In my defence, though, I must point out that the Castle Hill shoot does employ a small army of schoolchildren at the end of the season to pick up as many of the offending wads as we can. We line the children up across each of the fields over which we have shot during the season and, armed with black plastic bin-bags, they diligently complete their task. We also try to pick up the wads as we go through the season, but on a busy shoot day this is not always possible. I know this is not perfect, but it does at least demonstrate the Estate's willingness to minimise the issues. I also know that my son, Robert, uses plastic wads at North Molton and like us has a great collection team to remove them. To demonstrate the effectiveness of his picking-up process, Robert dug 'quad-trap' circles round particularly heavily used pegs that had been shot on for the previous eighteen years. The soil was dug out and then sieved. In the 102 circular holes, three metres wide by three metres deep, the average number of discarded plastic wads found was 1.5 per hole.

Continuing with the controversy over high birds, and whether it is cruel to attempt to shoot game birds at extreme ranges, I am aware that the BASC (British Association for Shooting and Conservation) and some in the shooting Press are trying to extend and expand the debate. I see this as something of a fallacy, for birds are shot at extreme range on virtually every shoot in the country. The birds themselves may not be high up, but can be shot over adjoining pegs, or even two pegs along. Thus birds are regularly shot at ranges of sixty to eighty metres – but it seems to me that this only becomes an issue when that distance is directly over a gun's head! We at Castle Hill defend our high-bird policy by the fact that firstly we attract top teams of guns, who are much more likely to kill a bird cleanly, and secondly we pride ourselves on the number, and quality, of the pickers-up that we employ. They quickly descend upon any wounded or pricked birds and ensure that they are dispatched as humanely and speedily as possible. We employ a team of fourteen or so pickers-up for every shoot day. Our normal bag is in the region of 500 birds and thus these essential men and women (along with their wonderful dogs) are busily employed throughout the day.

Though many shoots operate with far less pickers-up, I am confident that we ensure that the ground is covered rapidly and effectively. Angela, my wife, is part of our picking-up team and she confirms what I already knew: that all those involved take great pride in their important role and are professional and diligent. I firmly believe that we keep any cruelty down to an absolute minimum. I would suggest, and this won't make me popular either, that more birds are not picked up and thus suffer on a small shoot with just a few pickers-up, or none, than on large, commercial shoots. Of course it is in our financial interests to ensure that all birds are picked up, but I firmly believe that the importance given to the way pricked and wounded birds are dealt with says more about the quality of a shoot than any other element. I must say I absolute loathe the practice that we all know happens on some shoots, where a 'clicker' is used to count the shots and the final number of birds is estimated, with little attempt or concern to retrieve pricked birds. This is the sort of attitude that gives shooting a poor reputation and should not be tolerated.

Guns themselves also have a huge responsibility in this area and one of my pet hates is guns who do not finish off pricked birds with their second barrel. Any bird that is not killed cleanly with the first barrel should be given a second. I appreciate that on some occasions guns do think they have killed a bird outright but I also know that some guns act in what I consider to be a rather selfish and inconsiderate manner, which again reflects badly on our sport. My boss, Caspar MacDonald-Hall, sets a great example in this respect and on the admittedly rare occasion when he does not kill a bird outright with his first shot he will focus on the pricked bird with his second and this commendable attitude should be applauded. Strange at it may seem, this is a welfare issue and if our sport is to flourish guns must raise their standards in this area.

There is something of an obsession amongst what I would label the 'old school' of gamekeepers on numbers and percentages of birds shot. I realise that there can be many historic reasons for this and no gamekeeper wants to be in a position where he has to admit that a smaller percentage of birds have been shot over a season compared with previous years. Yet focusing on the numbers does not improve the quality of the shooting. Certainly on Exmoor the trend amongst guns is to look for high, quality, challenging birds to give them their thrills and their shots, if not always the bag. Indeed, on more than one occasion at Castle Hill, a team of guns has finished the day with half the bag they have paid for, but having fired plenty of cartridges. Never has one of these teams left us disappointed and all have rebooked for the following season. Yes, I will adjust drives if I feel the guns are struggling, but I will never produce 'bag-filling' drives as I believe this insults both birds and guns.

Nothing gives me more pleasure that flushing 200 or so birds over a team of guns, knowing that the birds are high but still in range, and seeing whether or not the guns can rise to the challenge. If not, they are still learning, improving their skills and enjoying doing so – and this thought also gives me a real buzz. Having said that, we often have days at Castle Hill when the guns exceed the stated bag, but we never consider an excess charge for this, as it is our responsibility to monitor the day. We never 'pull' a drive if the bag quota has been reached, but we do, on occasion, make sure the birds are in the air so at least the guns get to see them and don't experience the frustration of having the drive curtailed.

I appreciate that on many shoots the final bag is always the goal, but this does result in enormous pressures being placed upon the keeper and his team to deliver the numbers. Such pressure often means that the ability to focus on improving the birds or drives is lost. I know that some shoots provide the easiest drive at the start of the day so that a large number of birds are shot and the pressure to deliver numbers throughout the day is diminished. Myself, I would rather have a difficult drive first, not only to let me see how good the guns are, but also so that a full day's sport can be provided.

It is well known that I have had the odd difference of opinion with BASC, an organisation that in my opinion has done much good work for the cause and defence of shooting. Yet, as an institution, BASC has sometimes fallen into the trap of thinking itself to be infallible and that its utterances are almost divinely inspired. In the past it certainly has not reacted well to criticism of its work or actions. With the recent retirement of John Swift as chief executive, BASC has a new man at the helm, Richard Ali. Having recently heard Richard speak at the AGM of the NGO (National Gamekeepers' Organisation), I am positive that BASC will remain true to its central aim of protecting sporting shooting and the well-being of the countryside. Richard made it quite clear that he wants BASC to work with, and alongside, other shooting organisations, such as the NGO. This was nice to hear as BASC has sometimes in the past been guilty of going out on a limb with its views, and sometimes even against groups that should have a common cause and commitment.

My connection with BASC goes back several years and I am afraid the relationship has not always been harmonious. My good friend, Dave Clark (who is now HM The Queen's Head Keeper on the Sandringham Estate) and I, along with fifteen other keepers from across the country, were part of a gamekeepers' advisory group for BASC, which BASC decided to form after the demise of the old Gamekeepers' Association. We would journey to BASC headquarters in Wrexham roughly every other month for meetings. Our chairman, Ivor Beavis, who sat on the BASC Central Council, reported back to this body on our musings and deliberations concerning a number of issues central to gamekeeping. Whilst I am sure he did his best to make our views heard, his was something of a lone voice and Dave and I began to get rather disgruntled. I think the central problem was that BASC traditionally focused on rough shooting and wild-fowling and not on the commercial driven game-shooting that we were there to represent. In a sense this was, and perhaps still is, a cultural difference. Dave and I and our colleagues were giving of our own time to participate in the advisory group, and travelled miles to attend meetings, but we honestly felt that our findings and suggestions were not being given due consideration. These included our idea, which has since been put in place, of a dedicated phone-line to offer advice on gamekeeping concerns. It is certainly not the case that we did not put the effort in, or that we 'threw the dolly out of the pram' without giving the process every opportunity – after all, we were involved for more than eight years!

The final straw came after we had worked incredibly hard to organise two sporting auctions. Calling on every contact and favour we could, we put together some fantastic auction prizes and raised substantial sums of money (over £70,000 in one auction alone, held in May 1998). To our disbelief, although a certain sum was to be given to the Gamekeepers' Welfare Trust, we learnt that the lion's share of the money was not to be directed towards the three projects we had already identified as being of particular concern to gamekeepers, including a project for disease prevention, but was to go into BASC general funds. In retrospect, I think that BASC was concerned that, potentially, the 'tail was wagging the dog', and wanted to make clear who was running the organisation.

Dave Clark had thought for some time that the advisory board was not being listened to and had aired his views to the BASC Central Council. This resulted in Dave receiving a letter that ended his relationship with BASC. Now I, and four other board members, had had enough and we too resigned over the issue of how the monies raised entirely by us were going to be spent. The five of us – Dave Whitby, Terry Oscroft, Stuart Cannon, Alan Sefton and myself, nicknamed the 'Dave Clark Five' – duly signed a joint resignation letter with the intention of delivering it in person at our next scheduled meeting.

Matters often don't go as you have envisaged and this momentous resignation day was no exception. As we drove into the car park one by one it was evident that the senior management of BASC had, somehow, got wind of our intentions, for we were greeted by a line of men in suits, including the then chief executive of BASC, John Swift. It was soon apparent that this was a concerted attempt to persuade us individually to change our minds before the meeting was to start.

The five of us managed to extract ourselves from this initial interrogation and we convened in the meeting room. As soon as the Chairman called the meeting to order, I duly presented our signed letter of resignation and the five of us left the room. We were pursued out of the building and asked to reconsider, but we got in our cars and drove to a nearby hotel, where Dave Clark and Malcolm Fieldsend (then keeper for the Duke of Northumberland at Alnwick Park) were waiting for us. The mood was at first very sombre. I think we were all rather shocked and dumbfounded by events and by the implications of what we had just done. After twenty minutes or so, Dave aroused us from our stupor and made the suggestion that we should consider forming our own organisation that would really champion the concerns of gamekeepers. This sparked both our enthusiasm and our imaginations and we were soon chatting away, trying to decide on a name for this new body. Our first idea, the 'Gamekeepers' Organisation', soon became the 'National Gamekeepers' Organisation' (NGO), so as to give it a wider application. The five of us, plus Malcolm, decided there and then to put our money where our mouths were, so to speak, and we each put a hundred pounds into a 'fighting fund' to get our ideas moving forward.

Fired up, we all returned to our regions and sat on our phones, ringing around to try to get our local contacts together to form regional sub-committees. My brief was to cover Devon, Cornwall and part of Somerset. Our proposal for a new organisation was received very positively by all my gamekeeping colleagues. Eventually we had our first meeting in a public house near Exeter and I was astounded by the interest. More than seventy keepers from the region descended upon us and in no time at all we were up and running. This success was repeated across the country and very quickly all the regions were covered. To me this clearly demonstrated that there was, and is, a real need for the NGO. The Press was similarly supportive and in particular the then editor of the *Shooting Times*, Mark Hedges, really helped us on our way. Looking back, it is something of a shame that we had to go through the nastiness of a split with BASC really to understand the level of that need.

I was duly elected Chairman of our new, regional NGO, covering Devon and part of Somerset, and it has since become a major part of my life. Not that I begrudge this at all, for I believe that the NGO is making a real contribution to the welfare of gamekeepers, as well as helping to improve our understanding of all the numerous issues surrounding game shooting. In the long run, this can only benefit all who love and enjoy our sport. Our regional Chairmen met very regularly in those first few months, usually at a centrally located hotel in Staffordshire, and together we drew up our ruling constitution, which was based on the slogan 'Keeping the Balance'. Whilst our main aim was, and still is, 'To promote, improve and protect gamekeeping in the United Kingdom, thereby securing a thriving long-term future for the profession', under this broad heading we then specified many important objectives. We not only represent and assist gamekeepers, but also ensure quality within the profession by upholding both the codes of 'Good Shooting Practice' and 'Good Rearing Practice'. Finally, we believe that our role is to defend all field sports and we think that the best way to do this is to ensure that gamekeeping as a profession maintains the highest standards and quality as well as being well-represented. All this may sound rather long-winded, but the NGO's core principles are vital and need to be cherished. By doing so, I personally believe that we will show to those outside the world of shooting that we are professionals whose main concern is the welfare of the countryside.

In the seventeen years of the NGO's existence it has altered enormously, but has, I believe, stayed true to its central objectives. We now have a membership in the region of 15,000 of whom just under 5,000 are registered gamekeepers, all of whom have had to provide their employment details so as to confirm their eligibility. The remaining 10,000 or so are supporter or corporate members. We now have a very active website, a development officer, a welfare officer, a public relations officer, advice helpline and a solicitor's helpline. We are active in many debates on both shooting and countryside issues. We provide free members' advice sheets on such issues as the Firearms Act, game-rearing, shoot risk assessments and even advise on beaters' pay and tax matters. Basically, the website provides a place for its members to visit where help, advice and reassurance can be easily and readily found. Many of our members have a close association to Government (our National Chairman, Lindsay Waddell, has had lunch with the Prime Minister) and our voice is not only heard but our views are sought too, particularly by conservation bodies. We take our quality statement very seriously and if any of our members are proven to have broken either the laws of the land surrounding shooting or the Codes of Good Practice, then their membership is revoked. Sadly, this has recently happened.

I recall that just a couple of years after we had established the NGO, Tony Roff suggested at one council meeting that we should reinstate national pigeon shooting day, not only to deal with the pest of too many pigeons, but also as a means of raising much needed funds. For whatever reason, we were attacked in the most forthright manner by BASC. Its position was derided in the shooting Press, with some suggesting arrogance on the organisation's part. We, as the NGO, decided not to enter into the debate, which became more and more fractious as gamekeepers across the land wrote letters to the shooting papers in defence of the proposed pigeon day and critical of BASC's position. I am aware that several folk resigned from BASC in disgust. The matter was finally resolved with an apology from the then Chief Executive of BASC. As I have already mentioned, it is a huge disappointment when disputes become so heated, but I do sincerely hope that our two organisations can work harmoniously together for the future of shooting as a whole.

Another organisation to which I have formally committed is the Gamekeepers' Welfare Trust, which is so ably run by Helen Benson. Lord Alresford asked me to join the Board and I was happy to do so, for I passionately believe in the work that the Trust undertakes. Helen maintains a register of vacant positions whilst at the same time offering help, advice and counselling to gamekeepers who often need a friendly voice, for the job can be fairly lonely and incredibly stressful. The Trust is also able to offer hardship payments to both retired and current gamekeepers who might be between jobs. I am perhaps in a unique position, due to my involvement with the NGO and my longevity, in that I am in contact with the majority of keepers in the south-west and I am happy to assist the Welfare Trust in any way that I can.

There has only been one persistent critic of the 'Exmoor high bird' in the shooting Press. This individual, who writes for the *Shooting Gazette*, seems to have a particular agenda and has been somewhat vocal about the issue of pricked birds and large bags on Exmoor. I have rarely responded to this rather lone voice. I do, however, defend the practice of shooting at every opportunity. Perhaps surprisingly I have never had a confrontation or cross word with anyone who is anti-shooting. I may simply have been lucky. Over the years I have met many folk who do not agree with shooting but I have always tried to make an effort to have a rational conversation with them, stressing welfare and economic issues; and although we might not have come to an agreement, I have never had to raise my voice or had anyone raise their voice to me. I do feel that anyone who is involved in game shooting, at whatever level, should be an ambassador for our sport and must, therefore, control their temper and maintain their dignity, sometimes in very difficult circumstances.

I sincerely believe that the Exmoor high bird has opened a new chapter in the history of game shooting in this country. Whilst shooting is undoubtedly a national pastime, the rise of shooting in the West Country, and in particularly on Exmoor, has resulted in a geographical shift as to where the biggest and what are perceived to be the best shoots are located. Over the last thirty years, whilst some areas have raised their shooting profile others have declined and it seems clear to me that new parts of the country are trying to emulate what has been seen on Exmoor. North and South Wales, Yorkshire and the Scottish Borders all now have up-and-coming high-bird shoots to match those found in the West Country. I do not doubt that other parts of the country with the right topography will do likewise in the near future. Although at first the Exmoor shoots received criticism from the more traditional shoots – who saw a loss of bookings and business to us – I do not believe that Exmoor should feel threatened by the increase in high-bird shoots elsewhere in the country. Indeed, I strongly believe that the growth of such shoots, as long as they maintain quality, should be applauded and encouraged. Their wider existence will enhance and improve the shooting experience for all and furthermore will encourage change and better standards, whether this be in, for example, the type of cartridges used or picking-up skills.

I simply love my job, and one of the things that really stimulates my old grey matter is the fact that to make a shoot day work perfectly so many different elements have to be successfully combined. I have already mentioned cartridges, topography, pickers-up, but over the years I have come increasingly to realise that the quality of the birds themselves is what is so vital in producing a superior day's shooting. It is an area that I believe many shoots still neglect. There is far too much emphasis on the price of poults, with the frequently held belief that the cheaper the poult, the better the value is for the shoot. This, to my mind, is totally wrong and a false economy.

It was not until I was employed at Castle Hill that I myself had a 'road to Damascus' moment and the scales fell from my eyes. I realised that, even during my days at Miltons, we had become used to inferior birds. However, by utilising the latest thinking coming out of America and France, we had an opportunity to improve the quality of game birds dramatically. In the past, the reason for the poor quality of British game birds rested solely with game farms, in my view. Time and time again, I saw birds being held over for breeding stock for the next season invariably taken from the last, late hatching. Whilst this may have made strict economic sense, in that feeding and maintaining these birds would be less costly, this was a fundamental mistake. If a game farm had already put ten separate hatchings through the incubator system, the last batch would never be the best. Instead, the first hatched birds should have been kept back and over-wintered to provide the next year's breeding stock and thus produce better quality birds. However, this would have been at a greater cost to the game farm and few ever considered such a quality-driven approach. To use a comparison from the world of horse racing, you would not think of breeding the next generation of winners from the worst stallion but always from the best. Such a method unfortunately costs money and requires greater thought.

The lack of awareness as to the quality of birds extends to many shoots. It is frequently the case that the best quality birds, the ones that fly best, are the ones to be shot first; then the birds that are left at the end of the season tend to be the ones that have flown so poorly that they have been unable to be shot at! In addition, these inferior pheasants are allowed to breed amongst themselves to produce another generation of poor birds. This is why at the end of the season at Castle Hill we spend weeks in February and March catching the survivors and moving them well away from the Estate so that they cannot disrupt the following season.

It was around twenty-five years ago that I began to give some serious thought to the quality of British game farm birds. Whilst some companies were looking to improve and innovate, more were not. The introduction of breeding stock from Sweden and from captured wild Fen pheasants from East Anglia did result in a slight improvement, but once these birds had bred with our British birds for a period, the advantages were lost. It seemed clear to me that we would have to consider looking further afield for answers to quality issues and would have to take a close look at the selective breeding of birds, based on the superiority of specific breeds. Many in Britain saw this as a step too far but, in my ever-continuing search for quality, I turned first to America and then to France.

A company named MacFarlane, based near Janesville, Wisconsin, is a family-run game farm business, run on an epic scale. Each year, over 1.5 million chicks are hatched and around 400,000 mature pheasants are sold across America. For years MacFarlane has been at the cutting edge of a selective breeding programme, based on the genetic strengths of the birds. This is a truly dynamic, innovation-led business. From the mid-1980s I began to read of some of the improvements in quality that MacFarlane was claiming and I was naturally intrigued.

In America, due to the high number of predators, particularly birds of prey, pheasant shooting is very different from that which we see in Britain. Many American shoots operate a 'day release' system, in which the game birds are released from crates on the day of the shoot, or just a few days before, so as to minimise the losses from raptors, snakes and so on. This means that the birds have to be extremely strong and resilient. A similar system of release operates in large parts of France and it was French breeders who first travelled to Wisconsin to learn of the innovations at MacFarlane. Breeding stock was purchased and imported to France so as to improve the quality of the birds there.

Always looking to improve the quality of the birds at Castle Hill, I decided to import both eggs and chicks from those French game farms that had bred from MacFarlane stock. Considered a revolutionary, even treacherous, step by a few die-hards in Britain it may have been, but this was hardly going to stop me in my quest for improvement. Breeds such as the Kansas, the American and French Common have, over the past twenty years at Castle Hill, consistently shown themselves to be superior to solely British-bred birds.

Over the years we have developed a long-standing relationship with Ben Brown of Hardwick Game Farm, near Bury St Edmunds in Suffolk, a business established by Ben's father, Andrew. Ben imports chicks from France and we purchase them from him when the poults are six to seven weeks old, travelling overnight to minimise any discomfort for them. Hardwick's was first brought to my attention by John Marshall at Chargot, who bought all his pheasant and partridge supplies from them and could not praise the firm highly enough. That was all the recommendation I needed and now the vast majority of our birds are sourced from Ben's company.

One of the main reasons I buy from him, apart from the wonderful service he offers, is that the chicks are reared on the light, dry soils on which wild Fen pheasants have done well for centuries. It seems natural to me that birds reared on soils that suit them best will be superior, as they will have had the best start in life. This can only be of benefit to their strength and constitution over the coming season. I believe that game farms situated on the eastern side of Britain have a distinct advantage over those in the West Country, not just because of the lighter soils but also the drier climate. Anyone who lives in Cornwall, Devon or Somerset will know that we have more than our fair share of rain, driven in by the prevailing south-westerly winds. We often have to endure 'winter' storms in the spring and I can recall one cricket match I played on Exmoor in May that had to be stopped because of a snow-storm! Such conditions mean that perhaps only one year in five is perfect for pheasant breeding in the West Country. I know that some people, Alan Beynon included, maintain that game birds need a tough start in life to make them stronger adults, but I have to disagree. This is also an area of some contention with my son Robert, Head Keeper at nearby North Molton. For the last fourteen years or so he has reared pheasants on Exmoor, from day-old chicks sourced in France. I also know that other shoots, for example at Molland and those linked to the Angus Barnes Loyton Shooting Group, rear their own birds and naturally I wish them all possible success: but rearing birds myself is not for me.

In my view, each new batch of young birds should be provided with the best possible conditions to enhance their strength and quality and I am always considering how this can be achieved. I think even minor changes can make a difference to how a bird will fly once the season begins.

For example in 2013, learning from our experience of the extremely wet conditions of 2012, we decided to place crushed hardcore underneath the feeders in the release pens at Castle Hill so that the young poults did not have to wade through mud all the time to find food. This, I am sure, will have reduced our losses from disease and sickness by producing healthier birds.

To reiterate, I firmly believe that some British game farms

have a great deal of catching-up to do in terms of rearing top-quality birds. Perhaps the easiest and most effective step they could take, as I have said, would be to keep the first hatched birds, over-winter them properly and breed from this closed flock of stronger birds. Whilst there would be a cost to this I am sure the quality would improve. However, until we get away from thinking that a cheap poult is a good poult we will never see dramatic improvements in British-bred birds.

Before I am accused of being elitist, and having a budget that allows me perhaps to indulge my whims, I would like to point out that I am paying less for French breeding-stock poults than it costs to buy poults that originate on UK game farms. I would argue that these are bred from the inferior birds left over from the previous year. In addition, it is often the case that poults bought from game farms that have taken in 'caught' birds would have been bred from these old inferior birds and thus the rather depressing cycle is maintained and perpetuated.

For many years I knew of only one game farm in the UK that over-wintered its breeding stock and that was Home Park. I did once buy from there for Chargot and found the poults to be good, sound birds. Although more British rearers are now over-wintering their breeding birds, there are still too many that rely on late-hatch birds or caught birds. I do now buy some of my poults from a local game farm near Torrington in Devon, where they rear chicks imported from France; but I will not have birds bred from caught-up birds on the Castle Hill Estate and have not done so for more than ten years. As far as I am concerned, the superior quality of our shooting depends on the quality of the birds in the first place.

Whilst my comments may seem rather damning of British game farms, I would like to make it clear that many are now beginning to think of different ways of improving the quality of the birds. For example, some are using the 'raised' system of over-wintering, in which a cock bird will be placed with seven hens in a coffin-shaped box, raised off the ground, with a feeder at one end and a sheltered area at the other. This system protects the birds, and their eggs, from winter's elements, keeps them and their feet dry and stops amorous cock birds from damaging themselves by fighting over the hens. All this reduces stress and allows the birds to concentrate on successfully breeding better quality birds. It is a system that I believe is essential for breeding partridge in particular, as they are so susceptible to the cold and wet. Unfortunately the raised system has received some criticism from BASC, which has come into direct conflict with the NGO over this: BASC have argued for the more traditional, natural method of wintering birds in open flock-pens on grass. This seems to show a complete lack of awareness of the British weather, which frequently turns such wintering areas into muddy hollows, where disease can attack. Various studies, by both Government vets and even a Scottish university, have concluded that the raised system is not cruel to the wintering birds, but that indeed there are health and quality benefits. I believe that it is a cost-effective and relatively easy way to produce an increase in quality and those game farms that adopt the raised system must be considered forward-thinking.

Although I realise that I am fortunate to have the budget I have, I know that if this was ever seriously reduced there would be two or three things that would be non-negotiable in my mind. First and foremost would be the quality of the young birds. You cannot expect game birds to fly well if the main criterion for their selection is 'the cheaper the better'. Second, I would not skimp on the quality of food they are given. It seems to me that too often birds are fed with the dregs of corn, almost the sweepings off the floor. To use once more a comparison with top racehorses, these beasts are fed only the choicest hay for their owners and trainers know that they will perform better if fed well. My son Robert knows that if his partridges are to fly well on a shoot day, then they need what he describes as 'the Red Bull feed' for breakfast. Quality feed produces quality birds.

We try to use corn of a quality of at least seventy-two bushel weight (pounds per bushel). Even we have had to compromise occasionally and during the dreadful harvest of 2012 we were only able to obtain corn of sixty-eight bushel weight, for that was all that was available. The moisture content of the corn is also important, and should be down in the region of fifteen per cent. All this of course costs money. With that in mind I decided to form a feed-buying group on Exmoor, not only to keep feed prices within reasonable limits but also, crucially, to ensure the quality of the feed we were all buying.

Around six years ago I used to buy our feed from a number of different mills. To begin with, Ben Brown (of Hardwick Game Farm) recommended to me a feed that was milled near his farm, just outside Bury St Edmunds. I was keen to continue using the same feed when the birds were transferred from Suffolk to Castle Hill, for I believe continuity of food is good for the birds. This worked well until a large conglomerate, BOCM Pauls, who own the Marsden Feed Brand amongst many others, bought out the milling operation. Although BOCM initially kept the name of the feed I had been using, I was just not happy with the formulation. I thus turned to another small milling operation, this time near Southampton, owned by a gentleman named Phil Hembury. I bought from Phil for a couple of years until history repeated itself and BOCM again bought into the business. Once more I was not completely satisfied with the formulation of the feed under the new regime and this got me thinking about what was in the feeds I was buying and whether I could influence the formula, the quality and the price.

After a few months of ideas rattling around my head, I decided to invite several Exmoor gamekeepers together to discuss over a pint the benefits of forming a feed-buying group amongst Exmoor shoots. My colleagues did not take much persuading as to the sense and viability of establishing a buying cooperative: it wasn't long before the Exmoor Buying Group came into being.

Fortunately, my next-door neighbour, a gentleman named Kevin Roberts, runs a company called Three County Feeds, based in Tiverton; he was able to give me some very useful advice as to the best way forward. Although Kevin had never been involved in producing pheasant feeds, he had come across various feed-buying groups within the farming industry and so he was able to point out some of the 'dos and don'ts'. Kevin's advice was not just aimed at helping the buying group to obtain the best prices, but he also explained to me the cost structures so that both the buyer and the supplier could be happy with the prices agreed. He helped me to understand the importance of building a working relationship with the feed suppliers, who of course need to be able to make a reasonable profit from their businesses. All this was rather revolutionary: never before had the game-feed companies been challenged on either their prices or their feed formulation, let alone both. The whole game-feed industry had become something of a cartel, with all the big suppliers showing a uniformity of prices across their ranges and the country as a whole. I for one considered such a situation as unhealthy and ripe for a challenge.

As you have probably gathered by now, I love a challenge. The combined buying power of the Exmoor Buying Group now made us a force to be reckoned with. Initially our combined efforts saw the Exmoor shoots involved in the scheme buying around 2,000 tons of game feed per annum. Five years on, with internal growth and by bringing on-board more shoots, we are now (in 2014) up to around 3,500 tons. With the cost of the various feeds ranging from £300 to £400 per ton we have some serious buying power. However, it is not all about getting the price down; the formation of the buying group has much more significance in terms of quality.

Right at the beginning we asked a number of feed companies to give us their most competitive price for what they considered to be their best available feed. We then received samples of these feeds and asked a nutritionist to examine them to determine the ingredients. A protein level in the region of twenty-five per cent is the usual starting point, but the feed must also have the right balance of fish-meal, ash and fibre so as to give the birds the best start. The nutritionist was even able to tell us which part of the world the soya had come from and the precise quality of the wheat. Armed with all the relevant information, the members of the Exmoor Buying Group had an in-depth discussion: the likes of Dan Reynolds (Wellshead and Miltons), Angus Barnes (Loyton and Haddeo), Rob Mitchell (North Molton) and Bob Hunter (Bradley) all had a big input into the debate. Finally we decided upon the preferred formula for the feed we would all use and buy in bulk. We regularly send samples of this chosen feed away for laboratory testing, to make sure that we are buying exactly what we have asked for, the set formulation, and that it will do what it says on the tin, so to speak.

We hold regular Buying Group meetings to review the past season and discuss which feed companies we should invite to tender for our combined order. Apart from looking at the effectiveness of the group, at our most recent meeting we also took the opportunity to have a talk from one of Alan Beynon's vet colleagues about the disease and sickness problems that had been experienced over the previous season. On the advice of Alan and his team, we all agreed to introduce acids into both the feed and water supplies with the aim and expectation that these acids would lower the pH in the guts of the birds. This would have the benefit of increasing the nutrients that the birds could absorb whilst at the same time reducing the ability of pathogens to reproduce in the gut and cause disease. Such a modern, science-based preventative approach should result in healthier birds that will fly even more strongly. Again, this is an example of how science and nature can work hand-in-hand, for the welfare of the birds and to the benefit of shooting.

The buyers' group has looked in the past at possibly moving into the areas of the combined purchase of birds and also wheat but we decided that this was perhaps a step too far. However, I am very proud of what the group has achieved, more around quality than price, and I sincerely hope that it has a long-term future.

One very pleasant extra benefit of the formation of the organisation is that we now meet as a group of like-minded individuals, with a common cause, on at least three occasions a year. We take turns to arrange these meetings, usually held in one of the various shoot lodges, and after our business is done we retire for a jar or two, or three... This social interaction is not only good for the soul, but it helps bind us together as a group. As an adjunct to the buying group, my son Robert started the Exmoor Keepers' Challenge, a clay-shoot competition, held near Wiveliscombe this year, in April 2014. Twelve teams of guns, four to a team, blasted away trying to out-do each other and various silly activities took place, including trying to stay on a mechanical bucking bronco. I must admit that I excused myself from that, but time together at events like this not only reinforces our friendships but unites us more strongly in our profession, which can only be good for game shooting on Exmoor.

But to return to the birds: the whole issue of feeding them is a science in itself. Now that we have come to an agreement on the type of feed used across the group, when in the release pens we allow roughly two tons per 1,000 birds. Once released, around the end of July, we start feeding them 'old' grain, that is to say last season's grain crop, as an early season grain can be too acidic for the young birds. However, after recent disastrous harvests, 'old' grain is hard to find in the UK and we have had to import. Due to the quantities of grain we use (six to seven tons per 1,000 birds over the whole season), I have started to forward buy, becoming something of a commodities trader, focusing on forward and spot prices, in my little part of Devon!

We continue to feed the remaining birds after the season has finished and before they are caught up and moved away. This has been particularly true in recent years when wild food has been scarce. Although this may seem to be something of an extravagance, I do believe that it is the right thing to do; I would not want to see game birds starving after the end of the season and it also benefits the songbird population at a critical time for their survival. We certainly go the extra mile at Castle Hill to try to maintain the songbird population. Over this past year (2013-14) I have planted more than thirty acres of wild bird mix, which will be a huge benefit. I like to think that I have a 9,000-acre bird table!

To me, a healthy songbird population reflects the general health of the countryside. I believe that all game shoots have a part to play in supporting our wildlife. Several of the Exmoor shoots have been working alongside the Game & Wildlife Conservation Trust and the British Trust for Ornithology for many years and it is hoped that very soon we will be assisting them both to try to demonstrate that there are many more songbirds found on a shoot than off it. Of course we will need to find out exactly why this is so, but the ready availability of food and of the shelter and warmth provided by cover crops are surely factors. It is hoped that we can devise some sort of 'crib sheet' to be circulated across the country to shoots so that good practice can be understood and followed. I sincerely believe that intensive farming has decimated both the flora and fauna of the British Isles and that it is in areas where shooting is strong, and so important to the local community, that wildlife is flourishing. Unfortunately it does not seem possible, just yet, that we can work with the RSPB on this important issue as that organisation has, in recent years, for whatever reason, not wanted to enter into a dialogue with us.

In some people's eyes, placing tens of thousands of birds on a shoot, as we do at Castle Hill, may be considered to be a huge strain on the indigenous wildlife. For various reasons, many of which I have already discussed, I disagree with this viewpoint. Apart from eating the odd insect or bug that other birds might eat, the pheasant does not compete with the likes of the grass-eating rabbit. The food we put down for the game birds, is, of course, consumed by the wild bird population too. When I am feeding on a dark, miserable, cold winter's morning, I am pursued by hungry songbirds: they rely on the food we provide for their very survival. Indeed, the lack of natural wild-bird food over recent winters has meant that I have continued to put out food long after the end of the shooting season. Our cover crops also give food and shelter to birds and to large mammals such as deer. We have moved away from such crops as maize towards conservation game crops like barley and linseed; they still do the job for us but also offer a supportive environment to other species.

CHAPTER EIGHT

The Future of the Exmoor High Bird

Whilst I am not, strictly speaking, an Exmoor keeper now, I am physically close enough to the moor that I can see its highest parts on a daily basis. I spent several years working within its boundaries and my second wife, Angie, is Exmoor-born and bred, so there is no doubt that I have a strong affinity with the area. Indeed I recently returned to the area of my birth and where I had grown-up; and I must say that this visit served only to confirm my love and affection for Exmoor, which I really view as my spiritual home. Exmoor offers a beautiful landscape with moorland, woodland, farmland and valleys. The summer tourist can enjoy these wonderful settings and delight in the cosy pubs and tearooms, but for me – and many others from all over the world – Exmoor is synonymous with high bird shooting. Exmoor is the third smallest of the National Parks, at 69,000 hectares or

170,000 acres, and was designated in 1954. Around 10,000 people live in the Park, of whom approximately 7,600 are of working age, but it is an ageing population now with more people over sixty years of age than under forty-five.

Beyond the Exmoor National Park boundary, particularly along the southern edge of the moors, the topography of deeply incised river valleys running from north to south, which were formed by the retreating ice of the last Ice Age, provides wonderful opportunities for both high pheasant and partridge, which can fully utilise the prevailing south-west wind. A third of the land (40,000 hectares) within the Greater Exmoor area, which includes the Park as well as the outlying boundaries, is managed for game shooting. Many of the sixty-five shoots identified in 2008 as falling within the Greater Exmoor area have a world-class reputation for being able to deliver consistently challenging high birds.

Miltons, Chargot, Bulland and Molland are probably the shoots that immediately spring to mind, but there are so many other hidden gems on Exmoor and the sheer number of shoots demonstrates not only the wonderful shooting ground that Exmoor is able to provide, but also the extent of the demand for shooting there. Many may view the number of birds shot and the cost of shooting as extreme, but as Sir Edward Goschen, who has done so much to encourage shooting on Exmoor, recently said, these factors are 'horses for courses': clearly there is a market and a demand for the type and quality of shooting that Exmoor is able to offer. It seems to me that criticism often comes from folk who don't really understand what is at the heart of Exmoor shooting: despite the cost, I think it offers great value for money and a great experience. Booking levels, and more importantly repeat bookings, provide the evidence that the guns who shoot there think the same. Whilst the growth in prominence of the Exmoor shoot is a twentieth century occurrence, and this has been covered in a previous chapter, I believe the changes and developments that have produced the phenomenon of the 'Exmoor high bird' in the past ten years or so have been as extraordinary as anything that happened in the 1980s.

I first met Dr Nigel Stone, the Chief Executive of the Exmoor National Park Authority, in 2001, in rather trying circumstances. I attended a Defra meeting to discuss the then foot-and-mouth crisis and I took the opportunity afterwards to have an informal conversation with Nigel. If examined in isolation, the aims and purposes of our National Parks, which were laid out by the 1949 National Parks and Access to the Countryside Act, could be viewed as being directly opposed to shooting. These are:

1. Conserve and enhance the natural beauty, wildlife and cultural heritage

2. Promote opportunities for the understanding and enjoyment of the special qualities of National Parks by the Public.

National Parks also have a duty to 'seek to foster the economic and social wellbeing of local communities within the National Parks'. I strongly felt at the time that, because of the clear economic importance of shooting to Exmoor, the National Park Authority should be looking to promote the sport on Exmoor, or if not actually to promote it at least to discuss and debate the role of shooting within the National Park framework. Nigel seemed receptive to what I was saying and we agreed to follow up our discussion with a more formal meeting.

Via the regional NGO, and my friendship with local keepers, I tried to get some Exmoor keepers interested in opening a dialogue with the National Park Authority but initially I found them to be reluctant. They seemed unable to see any benefit in doing that and there was undoubtedly some suspicion, given the aims outlined above, as to what the Authority was really all about. However, I did manage to convince enough people to come along to the Exmoor National Park headquarters in Dulverton for the first meeting; I pointed out that it would be far better for keepers to be talking and in on any discussions than not.

I suppose some folk might be surprised that shooting is permitted to the extent that it is within the Exmoor National Park. It seemed to me that unless a formal dialogue was opened between the Park Authority and the world of shooting, we might find ourselves very much on the defensive. The initial meeting was very encouraging and since then our relationship, based on mutual understanding, has gone from strength to strength. The secret for us has been very much to focus on the positives, rather than letting others emphasise the negatives. Through an initiative from Hugh Thomas, we have gone on to form GESA (the Greater Exmoor Shoots Association), which represents all of us involved in shooting: it has at least an annual meeting with the Exmoor National Park Authority to discuss areas of possible sensitivity and conflict. I suppose GESA could be viewed as a type of pressure group but it is so much more than that – for it also concentrates its attention on guidelines and best practice, as well as effectively championing the economic and social positives of shooting on Exmoor.

So many benefits have resulted from the dialogue between GESA and the National Park Authority. For example, we cooperated to produce the Exmoor National Park's guidelines for the management of game birds within the Park, which was the first document of its kind. Now, I believe, its principles are being adopted by other Parks in which shooting takes place. The document effectively highlights possible areas of conflict, as well as describing best practice in a number of areas – such as the preferred placement of pens and cover crops, to avoid adversely affecting the ancient landscape and to help to conserve and enhance the special character and qualities of Exmoor. The guidance also provides advice on minimising disputes over public rights of way and bridleways; and it offers advice to shoots about planning permission requirements and stock density. Overall, it is a great example of a document that supports and enhances rather than dictates.

Personally, I try to be as proactive as possible when it comes to wildlife conservation and biodiversity when considering the planting of cover crops, the positioning of release pens and the wider environment of a shoot. As I have said, GESA (and particularly the shoots it represents) works alongside the National Park Authority in this important area of conservation. The greatest recent success story is that of the Heath Fritillary Butterfly, which is making a comeback from the brink of extinction on Exmoor and is now fully protected. This success has come about through the hard work and concerted efforts of a number of Exmoor-based folk and organisations.

Both GESA and the National Park Authority have also worked together to examine the social and economic importance of shooting on Exmoor, something that we all believe to be vital. From this collaborative work it is clear that shooting directly sustains at least 1,600 jobs on Exmoor, whether this be as keepers, contractors, rearers, game dealers, hotel staff or others. The economic importance of game shooting to the Exmoor National Park is without question. This is especially true during the autumn and winter months when tourists don't visit the park in any great numbers. The shooting industry keeps hotels, pubs (many of them serving locally-reared game) and other businesses going who, without this vital income earned at an otherwise quiet time, would really struggle. GESA has calculated that 25,000 local visitor nights per year originate just from activities linked to shooting on Exmoor.

Perhaps more importantly, much of the income generated by shooting is what has been described as 'sticky money': in other words, once on Exmoor, that money largely tends to stay there and be re-circulated, providing additional economic benefit. For example, local contractors who are employed by the shoots for hedging work or the planting of cover crops spend their wages in local shops or further invest in their own businesses whilst beaters' wages are often spent in the bars of local pubs. Every penny generated from shooting and spent in the locality is helping to support and maintain a very special and important community.

I know from speaking to my son Robert that in North Molton shooting is the biggest single employer in the parish by a huge margin. At the end of this last season (2013-14) Robert was able to go to the local hotel and confirm ninety-eight nights of bookings for next season. It is fair to say that without such reliable income many local businesses would not be able to survive the winter months, and thus not be around to offer their services to tourists in the summer. In addition, the planting of cover crops and rental of shooting rights is an important source of income to provide an economic return from the upland farms and woods. In the case of the North Molton shoot, the sporting rights over several thousand acres of ground, as well as the 300-odd acres of cover crops, contribute a significant source of income to local farmers and landowners. In addition, the shoot directly employs five keepers.

The GESA 2008 report's headline figure stated that the benefit of shooting to Exmoor's economy was in the region of £32,500,000 per annum, a hugely significant amount that has grown even larger since. In addition to the economic importance though, to me and others like me, shooting also gives Exmoor its indefinable feel, its very soul and identity, particularly during the season itself, rather like fox- and stag-hunting once did. Without the income and the way of life, Exmoor would be much diminished.

Beyond its great economic importance, shooting provides enormous social cohesion. I am thinking particularly of the many teams of beaters and pickers-up who turn out on shoot days. Again GESA calculated that, for every team of eight guns that shoots on Exmoor, there will be on average a further thirty-two folk engaged as pickers-up, beaters, loaders and keepers. Not only are shoot days usually great fun but they allow folk to socialise, reduce isolation for many, and also maintain and enhance levels of fitness and well-being. This is good for the souls of all who get involved and is something that should not be overlooked. For many, great social times can be had outside the shooting season too. As I have already mentioned, the intensity of the season means that you are often in the same people's pockets, so to speak, for a four-month period but then may not see them again for another eight months. This doesn't seem right to me and certainly at Castle Hill we arrange the Beaters' Ball every year, a black-tie event that provides a great opportunity for folk to socialise, to dress up and let their hair down. In addition we always organise a summer barbecue and again I see this as an important get-together. I know other shoots across Exmoor host similar events.

Whilst shooting has brought many economic and social benefits to Exmoor, this is not to overlook the fact that pursuit of the sport has caused some serious headaches for the Exmoor National Park Authority. It has had to deal with various complaints from local communities – for example when a new shoot has opened and folk suddenly find themselves surrounded by hundreds of pheasants on the roads or in their gardens, or when lead shot falls on to their roofs. There have also been some unnecessary incidents of bad practice when irresponsible individuals have acted stupidly, by shooting or poisoning raptors. On such occasions the National Park Authority has worked alongside GESA and taken a zero-tolerance view, as well as using the opportunity to reinforce the importance of Good Practice and Codes of Conduct.

The benefits of cooperation with the Exmoor National Park Authority were clearly demonstrated early in 2014 when the Authority was approached by the League Against Cruel Sports, who expressed their concern about the amount of shooting on Exmoor. The Authority officials did not take sides but made a good economic argument as to why they felt they could not support any action by the League. The Authority could clearly demonstrate that its stance was valid and one that fell within its remit of seeking to foster the economic and social wellbeing of local communities within the National Park. If it had not been for our years of successful dialogue with the Authority, the criticism from the League Against Cruel Sports might well have taken a different turn and had a different outcome.

Recent developments, and perhaps even the philosophy of Exmoor shooting as a whole, can best be illustrated by looking at the North Molton shoot and the Loyton Shooting Group, run by Angus Barnes. After spending time with me at Castle Hill, my son Robert returned to gamekeeping at West Molland where he spent two happy years. Eighteen years ago (in 1996) George Stucley, the landowner of the North Molton ground, approached Robert to see if he could establish and develop a shoot there. Naturally Robert jumped at this great opportunity and has not looked back since. Starting with partridges in early October, Robert and his team of keepers, beaters and pickers-up host nearly one hundred shoot days a season. The guns are frequently very wealthy individuals who travel from all over the world to shoot at North Molton. They are sportsmen and women, not those who just enjoy shooting, but individuals who are at the top of their game and are only interested in being challenged by high birds and perhaps even being beaten by them, only to return again and again. Despite the high numbers of birds involved in each day, as well as the cost of the shooting, Robert has managed to establish a very friendly, even egalitarian, feel to the shoot days, an atmosphere in which everyone feels involved and valued. Mirroring our shoot lodge at Castle Hill, Robert has constructed an area where the beaters, loaders and pickers-up all have lunch in the same place, with the guns close by. Reflecting what shooting should always be about, whether on Exmoor or elsewhere, there is no 'them and us': personally, I feel this is vitally important. Robert and I enjoy the informal, healthy competition between our two shoots and, despite some lively banter between us, I am so proud and impressed by how Robert has developed a truly world-class, top quality shoot at North Molton, but at the same time has been able to foster and retain a real Exmoor feel to it.

The Loyton Shooting Group began with the Loyton shoot, which was established by Angus Barnes's father in the 1970s. At first Loyton was a private shoot, but its history has been varied. It evolved to become a private shoot with an attached syndicate, then a syndicate and commercial shoot, and now it is private again, primarily offering commercial shooting. Loyton is blessed with several great high pheasant drives, with Swine's Cleave, Woodcock Corner and Lloyds being regarded as the pick of the bunch.

Angus took over the running of Loyton from his father, who remained supportive but took a more background role. At this point Loyton was a commercial shoot but was shared with a syndicate. Angus was holding down a full-time job in London but still somehow managed to run thirty shoot days a season at Loyton. He came to the view that to make a commercial success of Loyton, he needed to expand to offer further days and this spurred him on to look for fresh ground. He found this at Combe Sydenham and, with the help of his Head Keeper Pete Conachie, Angus started the shoot pretty well from scratch, although the ground had been rough shot over for a number of years. Realising that more financial input was required to develop the shoot properly, Angus found two potential investors, shooting men who were keen to move into commercial shooting. Thus a syndicate was formed, to invest in the pheasant-only shoot of Combe Sydenham. The two gentlemen concerned had shot previously at Haddeo, under Sir Edward Goschen, the founder of Haddeo and Pixen; but with a change of ownership they had lost their end of January slot and came to Angus looking for shooting opportunities.

Combe Sydenham is a heavily wooded shoot and is certainly not a classic Exmoor type with straight driven birds. The birds there are always doing something different – curling, sliding – but are rarely straight, which is due to wind currents coming off Exmoor hitting wind currents off the sea. Of the twenty-two drives notable ones include Bird's Hill and Eddie's Hole, although the top drive is probably The Folly, which can be exhausting to shoot. It is technically very difficult with no two birds the same, although Angus tells the tale of witnessing George Digweed shoot an eighty-yard pheasant from the hip, crossing his neighbour!

Combe Sydenham is also run as a commercial forestry enterprise, again adding some complexity to the management of the land, which requires some careful balancing. The drive called Isengard is one that was originally heavily forested. Angus and his team saw the potential of it and were delighted when a great deal of the timber was harvested and a natural bowl was revealed. The planting of a cover crop behind the remaining tree-line allowed for the establishment of the drive. Its name arose because when the foresters had finished their felling, as usual they had set light to the piles of debris of small branches that remained: the first guns on this new drive stood between these still-smouldering piles, smoke enveloping them. The birds came over at a great height but could just be seen between the gaps in the wafts of smoke. This gave a real *Lord of the Rings* flavour to the landscape, hence the name.

I visited Combe Sydenham with Caspar MacDonald-Hall several seasons ago. I watched one drive progress and was extremely impressed by both the quality and height of the birds. I asked Angus if I could borrow his radio so that I could speak to Peter, who was in the beating line. '*Well done, Pete, welcome to the big time!*' I teased him – but I meant the remark as a great compliment. What has been achieved from scratch at Combe Sydenham is a great credit to all those involved and demonstrates once more the determination to make the shooting upon Exmoor the best to be found anywhere. The shoot now employs five full-time keepers (including Peter's brother, Mike), again an illustration of the economic importance of shooting to the area.

Angus has in mind a clear philosophy behind the quality shooting that the Loyton Shooting Group provides. The fun element is something that has always been a big part of the day. When the new syndicate members invested in the business, they gave three reasons for their investment decision:

1. To have fun

2. To take something that is good and to improve it as best we can

3. To have fun

These are the 'three' key elements of what the Loyton Group is trying to achieve. Angus prides himself on the fact that things are done well, in an unfussy way, with the attitude that nothing is a problem. But above all, shooting should always be *fun*. This is so much at the heart of my own philosophy about shooting that I can only applaud Angus and his team.

Angus firmly believes that it is vital for each gun who arrives at any of the Loyton Group shoots to feel that he or she is very special and not on some sort of treadmill of days, drives and birds. He never wants to hear beaters or pickers-up saying, 'Oh, the team yesterday shot better,' or something similar. The keepers and beating team concentrate solely on the guns who are with them on any particular day and Angus, like me, believes it is the shoot's job to present and ensure a positive atmosphere. This is critical to the day's success and it is why he focuses heavily, perhaps more than others do, on all the elements of the experience.

Angus believes that the 'shoot day' should be regarded as a twenty-four-hour period, rather than the relatively brief time-slot of the actual shooting. With 'a day' consisting of four to six drives, it means that a gun may actually engage in shooting for just two to three hours. Looked at like this, the hourly rate for shooting becomes even more ridiculously expensive. Hence the Loyton Shooting Group has built a lodge to accommodate the teams of guns and provides a whole, twenty-four-hour package – comfortable accommodation, a great breakfast, good elevenses and a fantastic lunch, cooked by wonderful chefs, accompanied by stunning wines. I know that, as a keeper, when you wake up on a shoot morning and know that the weather conditions are not going to be right for you to deliver an outstanding day for the guns, this is hard because you want perfection. Yet you are dealing with a wild bird as well as the foibles of the weather so some days can be difficult. This is when Angus thinks that the whole package of the day becomes even more important. He is convinced that one of the simplest ways to improve a shoot is to address the other elements, which all combined together make a great day's shooting experience, and add immeasurably to the memories of the day even if the weather is conspiring against you.

As I know from my own experience of trying to supervise a number of shoots when I was at Miltons, the sheer numbers involved in the Loyton Shooting Group place a huge strain on how Angus manages his time. He is candid enough to admit that he has made mistakes and recalls one day in particular when he went to see three different teams at three different shoots on the same day and made all three feel unloved. He now tends to focus his attention on just one team per day. Similarly, Angus learnt a lesson from a gun who shot at Combe Sydenham about eight or nine years ago. The birds weren't flying very well and the guns were being very selective. Angus was getting rather anxious that the bag would not be reached and was standing behind the gun-line, hopping about with tension and worry. One of the guns noticed his anxiety and came over and said to him: 'You do realise that you are here to entertain us and not the other way around.' I suppose that this is a lesson all keepers or shoot managers need to learn about customer service. Things will go right or go wrong but you just have to try your best and aim to exceed the expectations of your clients. Angus firmly believes that even on a terrible day, with awful shooting conditions, as long as the team of guns has a reasonable understanding of the vagaries of shooting then you can still exceed expectations in other areas to make the day as enjoyable as possible. Some guns do have to be educated about conditions but most are delighted to learn as much as they can.

As I do, Angus finds the development of ground really fascinating and is very much aware of the constant need for change and adjustment. Shoots simply cannot rely on drives that have always been the mainstay remaining so for ever. Angus (more than I ever will be!) is keen on the use of statistics and he compiles figures on how many birds have been shot from each peg on each of the Loyton Shooting Group's shoots over each season, so that he can assess whether drives have altered or need adjusting. His Head Keepers now have iPads to enable them to produce all the necessary figures on a regular basis throughout the season. Angus will know the cartridge statistics on each peg and can examine these figures to see how each drive is shooting right across the line. Each drive will also be analysed as to how it shot with particular wind directions and air pressures.

Angus's busy life was further complicated by the expansion of the Loyton Shooting Group. Haddeo shoot folded and at the same time the lease for the Stuckeridge shoot and for ground adjoining Haddeo became available, resulting in three pockets of land with shooting rights coming up for auction. The Group put in bids for all three parcels and to Angus's amazement, and perhaps with a little disquiet, he discovered that the Group had been successful with all three tenders. Suddenly his responsibilities increased from three to five full-time shoots. Initially this was quite a difficult number to manage and resource but all have gone from strength to strength.

The Group also spotted the interest in partridge shooting on Exmoor and the partridge shoots of Edgcott and Challacombe have been brought into the Group too. The Loyton Group is an active supporter of GESA and a member of the Exmoor Buying Group and I for one really appreciate Angus's input and frankness on these bodies. There has been a great willingness amongst the founding members of the Group to invest and expand. Angus and his team have built up a group of fantastic shoots and with it a successful brand. Any profits made are ploughed back and invested into the shoots.

Angus has worked alongside Alan Beynon as I have, and he too is adamant that you cannot sustain and build a business that involves a bird whose existence and wellbeing relies on the use of antibiotics. The Loyton Group avoids prescription drugs as much as possible and last season (2013-14) their drug use was minimal. Often as a result of work done by Alan Beynon, in conjunction with what we are doing at Castle Hill, the Group's keepers are gaining a real understanding of the needs and requirements of pheasants and what we can and cannot do with them. Consequently, the breeding strains and strength of the birds have improved dramatically in recent years. Keepering, feeding and watering regimes have all altered for the better, as has the way the Group looks at disease prevention and control. I know that Angus agrees with me that this is firmly the Exmoor way.

The Loyton Shooting Group provides exceptional, admittedly expensive shooting. Everyone involved is very professional and very conscientious about the whole process from start to finish. As most shoots do on Exmoor, Angus and his team are constantly working on various projects to examine how the local flora and fauna react to the management of keeping game birds and a great deal of time is invested in assessing how to improve the welfare of the birds themselves. Shooting is not all about killing a bird, but also how to look after and rear that bird correctly, with as little use of drugs as possible: this is not just for the sake of the birds' health and wellbeing, vitally important though that is, but to ensure that the best quality birds can be sent over a gun line to produce the best shooting in the country.

Angus believes shooting on Exmoor is in good shape, with strong demand last season and healthy bookings going forward.

Despite the size and income of the Loyton Group, Angus has succeeded in maintaining the essential Exmoor feel on all the shoots: the welcome is warm and genuine and the birds are of the highest quality. I believe that the future is bright for Exmoor shooting with the likes of Angus involved.

The keepers on Exmoor are not looking to destroy the confidence or morale of the guns who shoot there. We may attract many of the best shots in the world, folk that like to be challenged, but as I have said there is absolutely no point in sending hundreds upon hundreds of birds over the gun line that are too high and out of reach. Yes, we want the birds to be extremely challenging but we also want them to be shot. For the ability of the guns we attract at Castle Hill, I like to see a ratio of six shots to every dead bird on a 500-bird or a 3,000-cartridge day. If we achieve that ratio, then I am happy and consider that I have done a good job. More importantly, I know that the guns will be content.

Exmoor keepers don't often leave to keeper elsewhere. They normally stay and they stay for a reason, for they not only enjoy the Exmoor life, but they also know how highly Exmoor shooting is regarded. I may moan if I have to go as far as Tiverton, but we get guns travelling to shoot from all over the UK, Europe and indeed the world. This is an illustration in itself that Exmoor is at the pinnacle of the shooting world. If Exmoor has given shooting anything, it is that it has produced a consistent product – high challenging birds – and an experience that is in demand all over the world. Yes, we are blessed with wonderful scenery and a topography that favours high birds, but we also provide great memories and entertainment, whether they be of cracking birds shot, the characters involved or the unique scenery. Our shoots provide a 'package' that draws some of the most successful people in the world to Exmoor. They revel in the challenge our birds provide and thoroughly enjoy showing this off to their friends, family and business associates. We must be doing something right for, without naming names, I know of one Exmoor shoot that hosts over one hundred 500-bird days in a season that had sold every day, and every peg of those days, for the 2014-2015 season by the first week of January 2014! Shooting on Exmoor is in good shape.

Shooting people are frequently very charitable and those that shoot and work on Exmoor are no exception to this rule. About twenty years ago, Tania Hussell approached me to see if the Castle Hill shoot would get involved in helping to raise a substantial sum for the redevelopment of the Village Hall at Filleigh. Caspar suggested the idea of organising a clay pigeon shoot in Surrey and inviting some of his many London friends and contacts. Many of the beaters and pickers-up and all the keepers from Castle Hill helped to set up the day, organising refreshments and so on. The event was a huge success and at the auction afterwards the generosity of the guns was superb: in the end we raised £15,000, which was a great kick-start to the fund-raising campaign. I somehow agreed to a sponsored leg-wax, which I can confirm was extremely painful! This seemed to capture people's imagination and raised a few more thousand for the pot.

One of my ideas for raising funds for worthy causes was to introduce the concept of the 'Four Big Drives', in which a team of guns pays several thousands pounds to shoot four of the top drives on Exmoor. Basically the guns are driven to Miltons, Haddeo, North Molton and Castle Hill and shoot one drive on each. I don't expect anyone who is involved in such days, whether beaters, pickers-up, loaders or guns, to finish the day with any spare cash in their pockets! All willingly sign up for these charity days and contribute massively in their own different ways. The last time we held such a day, over £80,000 was raised for the Game & Wildlife Conservation Trust and the Countryside Alliance. We would like to repeat the day again soon to obtain funds for the Greater Exmoor Shoots Association so that a study can be undertaken on the numbers and range of wildlife to be found on Exmoor shoots, in conjunction with the GWCT. We also put on outside/boundary days for charities and the Devon Air Ambulance, Round

Table, NGO, the Gamekeepers' Welfare Trust, various cancer organisations as well as numerous local causes have all benefited.

My rather competitive nature has been used very productively in terms of fund-raising. Ten years ago, at the West London Shooting School, I and a team of guns made a successful attempt to claim the world record for the highest number of rabbit clays shot in a day. Eight NGO members and loaders, four of whom came from Castle Hill including Peter Gould, shot 10,710 rabbit clays in eight hours. Each gun would shoot for ten minutes and then have a break. I arranged to shoot the last ten minutes of the eight hours myself. What I did not realise was that Peter had had a hand in proceedings and, even though we had broken the record and I had completed this last ten-minute stint, Peter persuaded the officials not to let me know! I kept on shooting and shooting, thinking that this was the longest ten minutes ever... The joke at my expense continued and it wasn't until I had been firing for more than twenty minutes, cursing and swearing under my breath and with the sweat pouring off me, that Peter finally allowed the last whistle to be blown. What a bugger that man is!

Another charity request allowed me some special moments with my son Robert. With the aim of raising funds for cerebral palsy research, we dressed in our keeper's tweeds and visited the seven National Parks in the country. At each spot we met a keeper or keepers from the area and received a great deal of media coverage, both regionally and nationally. This exploit raised a significant amount of money, with the bonus for me of spending time with Robert; we made many new friends too.

Back in 2002, just after the dreadful foot-and-mouth outbreak had ravaged the countryside, I helped and took part in a 'keeper's ride day', which was the brainchild of Robert Eggins, the then keeper at Haddeo. Robert's plan was that the keepers in and around Exmoor begged, borrowed or stole a horse to join the local hunt and went out with them for the day. Very few of the forty-three keepers who descended on the meeting place of The

Blackcock Inn at Molland had any experience of cross-country riding, let alone jumping or galloping, myself included. It was with some trepidation that I got out of bed on the morning of the hunt. My previous experience of riding was three mornings spent in the company of George Witheridge, Master of the Devon and Somerset Staghounds, walking and trotting along local country roads. At one point, we had passed a gateway where a rather large dog started to bark loudly. My horse bolted to one side yet I somehow managed to stay in the saddle. George considered that this represented adequate training for the local hunt! Our party included three keepers from Arundel and Petworth in Sussex, who had driven down to Exmoor with their own horses. Not only was this a very generous gesture on their part but it also meant that three of our intrepid party had some idea of what they were doing!

I have to admit that not all of our party of forty-three keepers left the car park of The Blackcock when we finally set out. The support we received was overwhelming though and there must have been over 1,500 folk there to cheer us off. Many brought sausages and other snacks with them to share with us, as well as a bottle of something. The drink was liberally passed around with the inevitable result that many of the keepers, whose horsemanship was already questionable, failed to venture further than the car park, but simply slipped or fell from their saddles well before the horn to begin was sounded. Even with the odd casualty, over 200 horses did leave The Blackcock, which was quite a sight.

Sadly, the actual day was very foggy so the Master decided to try to ride up above the fog and we ascended Molland Moor. As we reached the top, the fog did indeed clear and much to my amazement we were greeted by the sight of a further thirty horses from the Devon and Somerset Staghounds who, due to the fog, were unable to hunt so thought they would tag along with us. Seeing so many horses together in one place was truly remarkable and it is an image that will live with me forever – it was a real country spectacle and to be a part of it made me feel very proud.

Of course this whole event took place well before the passing of the 2004 Hunting Act. We all rode together across Molland Common in search of a fox but the miserable weather meant that even our prey seemed to have had the sense to stay indoors.

By three p.m., after several hours in the saddle, it was clear that my experienced old hire horse, I think he was called Napoleon, was enjoying himself much more than I was. I was wearing my keeper's suit, which I soon discovered was not ideal and certain areas of my anatomy were starting to get rather uncomfortable. At the very moment when I was ready to give in to the pain, which was making me feel as if I was on fire, hounds suddenly caught the scent of a fox and gave tongue. The sound re-energised my horse and, unable to control his excitement, I was caught up in the mêlée of the chase. I held on for dear life, unable to steer or stop my mount and I have to say that it was one of the scariest experiences I have ever suffered. We pursued the fox for well over an hour before hounds did eventually manage to catch their prey. By this time it was dark but I managed to find the right horse box and I gingerly dismounted. I was able to grab a lift back to The Blackcock to join the other survivors of the day and we had one hell of a night, drinking and reminiscing about our experiences. Not only was the day a memorable one but also it was incredibly successful, in that we managed to raise over £5,000 for the Devon Air Ambulance, £5,000 for the NGO and a further £5,000 for a local charity. Again, this just goes to show how generous shooting and country folk can be. There was a price to pay though and when I awoke next morning my whole body screamed in pain with a combination of too much drink and far too long spent on a horse. I can't say that I have avoided drinking over the succeeding years, but I have certainly had the sense to avoid horses!

I have recently been asked to represent gamekeepers on the Police Firearms Liaison Committee for Devon and Cornwall, which is not only a huge honour but also a wonderful step forward in terms of greater co-operation between the police and the world of shooting, whether game or clay. As I have described earlier, I am also on the board of the Gamekeepers' Welfare Trust. Since 1992 this organisation has helped many gamekeepers, both current and retired, who have found themselves in poverty or distress. I was soon involved in my first decision, to provide funds for a specialist chair for a gamekeeper who had been paralysed in an accident at work. I am certainly committed to helping fund-raise for the Trust and indeed I was able to hand over a cheque recently for money raised from various charity events at Castle Hill during the 2013-14 season.

Someone who has shot regularly at Castle Hill for more than thirty years, and who has become a good friend of mine, is a gentleman named Bob Sperring. Bob has seen some significant changes in the world of shooting and he recently shared with me his opinion on Exmoor shooting. He has been very fortunate in that he has shot all over Britain and the world but he told me that he considers the West Country, and in particular Exmoor, as the mecca of shooting. The consistently high demand for Exmoor days would clearly suggest that others think the same. Exmoor shooting has survived, if not even grown, during some severe economic recessions and I sincerely believe that this is due to the quality of the shooting there. There is an old saying, 'class will out', which clearly applies to Exmoor shooting.

The sport is now represented by so much more than Miltons or Chargot or some of the other big-name shoots, fantastic as these high profile shoots are. Their success has inspired a real shooting culture upon Exmoor, which has drawn guns to the area from far afield. This in turn has brought money to the National Park and its immediate surroundings, allowing for the development of other shoots. The Loyton Shooting Group has already been discussed in some detail but there are now over sixty-five high-quality, driven game shoots on Exmoor, all contributing in their own way to the economic and cultural life of the National Park. Some may be well-known, such as Withycombe, which neighbours Miltons. Its twenty drives, including Burrow Wood, Riddler's Garden and The Punchbowl, all offer stunningly high birds. Others, perhaps less well-known, include Lillycombe, which has twenty-nine pheasant and partridge drives including Pitt, Dry Bridges and Up About as its signature drives. The 1,000-acre Melcombe shoot has been described as a 'boutique' shoot by its owner, Chris Kirby. The joy of a day there is the exceptionally high birds, the unique atmosphere and the stunning scenery. Wellshead, located near the village of Exford, is a similar shoot, spread over 2,000 acres with fifteen drives: Hill Cleave and Bennets present the highest birds on this shoot. Wellshead is far removed from what many outsiders would perceive as the normal high-bag Exmoor commercial shoot and offers an almost 'family shoot' feel. Equally hospitable is Great Bradley, where my old friend, keeper Bob Hunter, presents high birds from the wonderful valleys on this 400-acre shoot. Nestled between Miltons and Haddeo, the 1,000-acre Hollam shoot again produces exceptional birds over three deep valleys. Its signature drive, Carriage, sends birds forty metres in height over the guns.

It is impossible to mention all sixty-five quality shoots on Exmoor but the likes of Liscombe, Wood Advent, Buttery, Westermill and Mornacott all have wonderful reputations for quality and hospitality, as do so many others. GESA's 2008 survey found that the average shoot lets out only twenty-five days per season but that forty-one per cent of the Exmoor shoots set out to make a profit, with the bulk of monies earned being re-invested in the shoot and on Exmoor as a whole. Exmoor shooting may perhaps be regarded by some as elitist, exclusive and expensive but the amazing and significant rise and success of the smaller shoots in the area in recent years is testament to the fact that 'the product' is one that is well received. These smaller shoots, by offering days of perhaps 200 or 250 birds, are also more financially accessible to a wider range of guns than the larger ones. In general, all the shoots offer good value and 'bangs for your bucks' – and I am sure they will continue to do so.

The wonderful topography of Exmoor undoubtedly gives us a head start but our success is firmly centred on the people who work so hard to make each shooting day as good as it can possibly be. I hate this phrase, but I think those associated with Exmoor shooting have succeeded in building 'an exclusive quality brand'. Standards are high, the guns' expectations equally so, and by commitment and graft I believe that the area has earned its rightful place as one of the best places to shoot game birds anywhere in the world. Those of us who are associated with the shooting scene on Exmoor are indeed privileged.

CHAPTER NINE

Legacy and the Future

Many people probably think that I am slightly mad in that I actually enjoy getting up at four a.m. Yet I consider myself privileged to be out and about in the countryside at this time and to have it all to myself! I take pleasure from every season, but particularly relish the early morning light of May, June and July. One sight that reassures me that we must be doing something right in our little part of the world is the return of hares in significant numbers, for I believe that this animal more than any other is a real sign that the balance in the environment is returning to what it should be. Only the other day I saw sixteen hares in one field close to my house, which is a truly wonderful thing to behold. Similarly we have recently seen the return of a number of young stags to the vicinity; they are an awe-inspiring and reassuring sight. I can even go out of an early morning with my eight dogs and these stags will watch with total unconcern as we go about our chores, for they know that we present no danger to them. Autumn for me means wonderful colours, rutting stags, gathering swallows and swifts, and pheasants on the ground. Each morning is magical and different and I love every single one!

With the job that I do, the first few drives of a new season are always stressful as I wonder how the birds are going to fly. Then there is a feeling of huge relief, mixed with pride and satisfaction, when all goes well and the long hours and hard work prove to have been worthwhile. That feeling never changes but, as you can imagine, I *have* seen many significant changes in gamekeeping and game shooting in my nearly fifty years. I suppose one major change that has been very positive is how gamekeeping as a career is now perceived. In my day, and perhaps until recent years, young people almost fell into the role because they liked being outside and had few other attributes. This is not to denigrate anyone and many fantastic keepers have started off because there were few other opportunities and they simply took the job, only to find that they loved it and could make a full-time career from it. Today a number of colleges offer courses and qualifications in game management and more and more young people are attracted to gamekeeping as a career, although the long hours and physical nature of the job will not appeal to all.

In my experience, the position of Head Keeper now encompasses many elements, not just the rearing of birds and the organisation of the shoot day, but staff management and motivation, hiring and training and accounting skills, as well as land and forestry management. Of course running the shoot day itself is hugely challenging and on a large commercial shoot this may have to be repeated fifty, sixty or a hundred times in a season. I view my job as running a very diverse and exciting business and this does appeal to many. I suppose the biggest change during my own career is that gamekeeping is now a much more proactive rather than reactive job, as an example in the area of disease prevention. The job can still be a very isolated one, but organisations such as the NGO have helped to reduce this.

Certainly in the past gamekeepers had a poor reputation, as individuals who might be prone to accepting kickbacks or bribes and perhaps this, to me totally unacceptable behaviour, was driven by the relatively low wages that gamekeepers historically earned. Personally my integrity and honesty is everything to me; and this of course extends to anyone who works alongside me at any level. I do like to encourage a little healthy competition, or even rivalry, amongst my beat-keepers but I frown upon any beat-keeper who might be 'pinching', i.e. trying to entice birds from others' drives onto theirs. For me, that sort of behaviour goes too far and I would not tolerate it.

There is no doubt that my chosen career has taken a toll upon my body, although considering what I have asked of it, it is perhaps surprising that I have not suffered more. I have had both knees replaced, one when I was fifty-eight, the other at the age of sixty-three. The syndicate kindly paid for me to have both operations done privately in Exeter so that I did not have to wait. For all the miles I have walked and the cricket I have played, I put the condition of my knees (which the consultant eloquently described as 'buggered') down to the hours spent on the quad bike, or Polaris. For over twenty years, nearly every day, I have spent hour upon hour speeding around the countryside on a quad bike and, no matter what wet-weather gear I have worn, my knees have been exposed to the damp. It was arthritis, rather than wear and tear, that meant they had to be replaced. Indeed the pain from my knees became so bad at one stage that I had to use the Polaris to get around the shoot and I understand that the beat-keepers referred to this machine as my mobility scooter: cheeky buggers! Fortunately, although I have had my fair share of back problems, I have never been hindered by them for any length of time, despite the number of bags of feed I have shifted over the years. Swimming has been an important part of my life in recent years and I have really noticed that this has helped both my core strength and flexibility. I am not as deaf as many older gamekeepers and I count myself lucky in this regard as I did not really look after my hearing in the early years. Now, though, I never go anywhere on the Estate without my ear-defenders close by.

As you will have gathered, I firmly believe that both the welfare of shooting and the countryside are inherently linked. When I was a young lad everyone seemed to be so much more connected to the ways of the countryside than they are now; many kept chickens or bees, grew their own vegetables, caught rabbits and poached the odd pheasant. Today that connection is fast disappearing. Years ago, many of us worked in farming or, at the very least, had a family member or close friend who did. Again that link is fading. Even those of us who are lucky enough still to be living and working in the countryside are seeing an environment that has altered significantly from a mere twenty-five years ago: a countryside that is almost devoid of rabbits and deer in many areas, that has meadows with no weeds to attract butterflies and other insects is an environment that is alien to many of our species of animals, birds and insects and is in danger of becoming sterile. I am not saying that the countryside should be a museum but observing that it has changed beyond recognition and that we have lost our connection to it. I believe this is very dangerous.

Whilst this loss of connection is a particular threat to the pursuit of shooting – for many folk simply do not understand the economic importance of shooting or its valuable link to the countryside – I believe the sport presents a wonderful opportunity for us to return some of the missing elements back to the countryside. If shooting can restore our love, respect and enjoyment of the countryside to us, that has got to be of benefit to us all, whether we live and work in a rural or an urban setting. At Castle Hill, as I have said, we attract some of the most successful people in the world who make the long journey from their offices down to Devon. I can observe the gradual fading away of the stresses and strains that these folk have been under in their working lives, as they stand surrounded by some of the most beautiful and stunning scenery our country has to offer. They certainly appreciate and value the countryside at these moments, as do our loaders, beaters and pickers-up, all of whom simply adore both their roles and their surroundings. To restore and enhance this connection to the countryside is a vital contribution that the world of shooting can make and it is so important that it does.

Of equal importance is that the shooting community demonstrates that our sport does benefit the wild songbird population, with all the pluses this brings to everyone. If we can do this, then we can lead the way in bringing back some of the crucial and universally good things that have been lost in the countryside. By helping the flora and fauna of the British Isles to thrive, we will increase our love and respect for our environment and produce the strong connection to it that is good for all our souls. This, in my opinion, is by far the best means by which we can defend our sport for future generations.

Quality driven shooting (and some Exmoor shoots are guilty of this) is not about shooting a hundred or more birds, some of them ordinary, on the first drive, so as to take the pressure off the keeper in producing the agreed bag total. As I have said more than once, I do not see the job as purely a numbers game. My task is to present challenging birds, the kind that the sportsmen who come all the way to Castle Hill expect to see. If the target bag is reached, that is great: but if I show plenty of fantastic birds and the guns fire 3,000 or 4,000 shots in a day at them, then I have done my job well. Of course I do have to manage the numbers so that Castle Hill's paying guests can achieve a 500-bird day whether they come in the first week of November or the last week of January. This is not an easy task, but the folk who shoot here expect nothing less than the best and it is my job to deliver.

I think many people who object to large commercial days lose sight of the fact that quality shooting is about so much more than numbers. Such days are all about quality and challenge and that is what I wish to see as the hallmark of shooting on Exmoor: no bag fillers, just the best. I have witnessed excellent shots humbled by the birds we have sent over them, but rather than being deterred they come back for more. They really appreciate the ultimate test provided by top-quality sporting birds. Flinging undemanding birds over the gun line may be what some keepers and shoots out there still see as their primary purpose, but they are wrong. As guns become more astute and rightly more demanding, such shoots will fade and die as their customers vote with both their feet and their wallets. Quality is everything and if we lose sight of that we risk the future of the sport, for quality is remembered long after the price is forgotten.

I have been very encouraged in recent years by the increased demand and growing popularity of game birds as a foodstuff. Whilst pheasant and partridge have always been seen on the menus of Exmoor pubs and restaurants, their inclusion on menus right across the country is much more widespread. A great deal of effort has been put in by BASC and the NGO to encourage this. Many supermarkets now stock game, as well as providing recipe suggestion cards. Of course our sixty-odd days shooting at Castle Hill each season result in a large number of dead birds. For a number of years these were sold to game dealers in Belgium and Holland, but these outlets have rather dried up of late. We now sell to a national game dealer, Peterborough Game, run by Richard Bennett. He gives us a reasonable price for the birds and his company's fleet of refrigerated lorries and transit vans collects the game from quality shoots from Scotland down to Cornwall. We provide the dealer with a product as free-range and organic as we can deliver, and I know that Richard has been delighted with the quality of our birds. He supplies over 600 restaurants and more than 400 independent butchers, as well as wholesalers. Game birds are also exported to Europe, the Middle East and even Japan and last season Richard's factory processed over a quarter of a million pheasants bought from UK shoots.

At the other end of the market, birds that are not of the

highest quality enter the pet food market, with, for example, even skin and bones being used in the production of dog chews. Richard even has a market for all the feathers that are a by-product of the meat processing. These are compressed into sausage-shaped bricks and sold to a power station close to the processing plant: there the bricks are burnt in an incinerator to produce electricity!

The consumption of game should be encouraged as much as possible, although this should be done responsibly. No one wants a situation in which an individual becomes seriously ill from eating game from a source that has not handled or processed the game hygienically. Such an incident could ruin years of hard work in an instant. Much has been done in recent years, but I sincerely hope that the day will come when eating game is as popular as eating chicken. If this can be achieved, we will have done much to defend the sport of game-shooting as well.

It is up to a gamekeeper to provide great memories from a great day's shooting as well as the shooting itself. I believe that it should be so much more than just the time spent on pegs. For example, I really dislike it when guns want to shoot through and not stop for lunch. Socialising with like-minded people over lunch is a vital part of the whole package. Friendships are not made forty yards apart on pegs, they are made at the lunch-table. Over the years I have witnessed busy people rush down to the West Country to shoot and then disappear after the last drive, claiming that they are too busy to stop for a meal. They will have missed out on one of the most pleasurable parts of the shooting day, returning to their hectic lives almost as stressed as they were when they arrived. Lunch brings friendship, camaraderie, banter – that all-important social aspect to the day. To my mind lunch should be compulsory!

As the cost of shooting ever increases I am concerned by two factors. First, there seems to be a trend for some shoots to move away from 150-, 200-, even 250-bird days, to days of 400 or more birds. Whilst I can easily understand the financial rationale behind this, I worry that an already expensive day will become prohibitively so to many guns. Whilst demand for shooting on Exmoor from foreign guests has remained strong, I do think it is important to still attract, entice and retain teams from the UK. As I have said, a day's shooting is about memories and for the guns a memorable and thoroughly enjoyable day can be had with any number of birds, as long as the quality is present. My second big concern is the lack of land available for rough shooting. I have such fond memories of hours spent in my childhood and youth out walking the fields near my home in Dorset, under the supervision of men who really understood the countryside. These hours gave me both my love of the countryside and of shooting and so greatly influenced me. As I say, there seem to be fewer and fewer opportunities for young people to enjoy rough shooting and there must be a real danger that this will result in fewer guns in the future.

The shooting of game birds will only continue in this country if we can encourage young people to take up the sport. I have always made a real effort to involve youngsters, from the earliest age, in helping out around the shoot. Dave Sexon is a prime example of someone who started his career in this way. This year we have had three school-leavers with us on a week's work experience and another for three weeks from Sparsholt College near Winchester. I can only hope that all four of these individuals take away with them a growing interest in the countryside from the time spent with us.

I have never been slow to encourage youngsters to pick up and fire a shotgun. Some argue that there should be a minimum age before children can be close to or handle shotguns and there was even a rather silly attempt a few years back to place an age restriction by law on youngsters going into gun-shops. Not only is such talk a complete waste of Parliamentary debating time, if such a law was in place I am convinced it would make shooting more, not less, dangerous. Youngsters need an awareness of guns from an early age so that they treat them with respect and are not tempted to handle or view them in the wrong way.

We did host for a number of years what I referred to as 'boys' days', although girls were invited too! On these occasions, local farmers' sons or daughters or the young of folk who helped most on the shoot or Estate were invited to shoot at Castle Hill. The days were highly regimented and controlled with each lad or lass being assigned an instructor who would also load for them. Everything was very safe and very legal and the days gave the youngsters the opportunity perhaps to fire a shotgun for the first time. Any mystery or misconception about the guns and the sport were removed. Their parents or non-shooting siblings would usually offer their services free on the day as beaters or pickers-up. I suppose each gun had an opportunity to shoot perhaps two or three birds in the day, and some did connect, but this was not the main point of the exercise. I recall these outings with great fondness, for it was lovely to see the different generations out together in the countryside. I also know for a fact that many of these youngsters subsequently worked at Castle Hill and now have their own shotguns. I do hope that we can reinstate these days again soon, for not only were they great fun and a magical experience, but such events can only foster a love of the countryside.

Scientific study of the diseases that affect game birds and the influence on them of the birds' environment, is an area of gamekeeping that has come on leaps and bounds in recent years. The effective use of scientific knowledge can be a legacy for those gamekeepers who come to the profession after us and it can be used as an effective tool to reduce or even nullify the criticism that game-rearing and shooting is inherently cruel.

After many conversations with our vet Alan Beynon, we were inspired to produce a long list of all the factors on the game farm, in the release pen and out on the shoot that can negatively or positively affect the health of the birds. So, for example, we came up with twenty or so factors that are important influences on the likelihood of disease occurring in release pens. We then looked at all the pens to see if these factors were present. The analysis included such details as the breed of pheasant, where it was bred, if it came from a game farm or was reared on the shoot, where the feeders were located, access to water, wildlife interference, weather conditions when the poults were delivered and so on. We then looked at the incidence of disease in these pens to see if there was a link. We are now extending this idea to all areas of the shoot and, in combination with two or three other shoots and their vets, in other parts of the area, we should be able to develop a computer program that covers every pen that Alan and his practice team visit. Then we can build up a comprehensive picture of any disease and welfare issues and decide what needs to be done to rectify or improve them.

Some reluctance has been shown by the game farms to take part in our study, but slowly Alan and I are convincing these good folk that the blame culture has gone and that the information we compile will be for the benefit of all of us in the long term. This is a two- to three-year project and after it is completed it is hoped the information gained can be shared nationally via a computer program or direct internet access. (Alan is also working on a similar, but separate, project looking at partridge.) This is a really exciting and dynamic initiative that will again demonstrate to the outside world our total commitment to the welfare of our game birds.

I was recently much cheered by comments made by the RSPB's (Royal Society for the Protection of Birds) Conservation Director, Martin Harper, at the 2013 CLA Game Fair when he was quoted as saying:

> *'Shooting can do some fantastic things for our wildlife... There are loads of people doing some great things with shooting at the heart of their land and wildlife management.'*

Positive stuff. Yet within just a few weeks of his remarks, the RSPB issued a press release claiming that the decline in hen harrier numbers could be directly attributed to the management of grouse moors. The RSPB has also been vocal in its criticism of the release of pheasants on the basis that they are 'non-native'. I suppose the RSPB does find itself between a rock and a hard place, in that it knows that very good work is being done by the shooting establishment, especially gamekeepers, in the area of wildlife conservation, yet the majority of its members will be opposed to game shooting. This in itself is something of a tragedy, for if this conundrum could be resolved then the resources and infrastructure of the shooting world and the RSPB could surely be combined to the benefit of British wildlife as a whole. I firmly believe that the leadership of the RSPB needs to explain robustly to its members that a well-run shoot helps support and conserve our precious wildlife. At the same time, I will resolutely support the RSPB when it highlights the failings of wrongdoers who jeopardise the natural environment.

It is more important than ever that the shooting world strictly adheres to its own codes of good practice if a serious and constructive dialogue is ever to be opened with the RSPB. With this in mind it was very disappointing that no shooting bodies, no BASC, NGO or anyone else, were invited to contribute to the RSPB-led *The State of Nature* report, which was released in May 2013. The report – a collaboration between twenty-five conservation and research organisations but, as I say, not one shooting body – clearly showed that our wildlife is in trouble. As a slight aside, I think that it is incumbent upon all shooting organisations to ensure that any reports they release are, beyond question, solidly backed by credible research. I am not saying that this has not been the case in the past, but we must ensure that it certainly is in the future, if our voices are to be heard clearly and viewed as more than the utterances of a pressure group. As time passes and as long as we continue to demonstrate that our words are scientifically based, then it is more likely that we will be able to enter into the important general debate on all issues surrounding the countryside. If we do this and are still excluded from any involvement in a report like *The State of Nature* then we will have every right to voice our disapproval forcefully, vocally and at the highest level.

The current position of over 6,000 species was assessed in the report and it was revealed that more than one in ten are thought to be under the threat of extinction in the UK. The performance of 3,148 species of British animals and plants was quantified by comparison with previous academic studies, some of which go back over fifty years or more. Sixty per cent of species had declined, with thirty-one per cent showing a marked reduction. The report stated that the country has lost 44 million pairs of breeding birds since the 1960s; that in many counties a plant becomes extinct every two years; and that seventy-two per cent of butterfly types have declined in the past decade alone. Clearly our wildlife is in crisis.

Unfortunately the report focused in two sections on the conflict with the world of shooting. For example, under the subject heading of *Illegal Persecution*, the report states: '...hen harriers and other raptors are killed throughout the UK due to perceived conflicts with game hunting interests.' Furthermore, the section that concerns *Upland Management Habitats* states that: 'Bogs and mires have been drained and habitats damaged by intensive burning for managed grouse populations.' Whilst there are serious concerns in both these areas, it is disappointing that shooting bodies could not have been involved in the report too. I for one would not criticise the RSPB for this but would simply point out it was a missed opportunity. Such general, sweeping attacks on grouse-moor management and game bird release do nothing to resolve instances of general mismanagement.

Of course I, and most people involved in shooting, would be happy to work with other organisations to root out bad practice and even illegality; perhaps we need to be shouting that out a bit louder. Mutual confidence and respect is much needed between the world of shooting and bodies such as the RSPB for, fundamentally, we are all striving to maintain and enhance our wildlife and surely that can better be achieved by working together? I was delighted that Martin Harper of the RSPB accepted the invitation from the NGO to speak at our seventeenth AGM in April 2014. This in itself was a very positive step and I applaud Martin for stepping into 'the lion's den'. I know that many keepers appreciated the fact that Martin agreed to talk to us and much respected the effort that he made.

I must say I also agreed with much of what Martin had to say. He recognised the economic importance of shooting interests to many landowners, estates and regions. He went on to say: 'It is only through talking that we get to understand each other a bit better and that is a prerequisite for any collaboration. A battle of dogma or a war of words conducted through the media helps no one.' I could not agree more. In addition, Martin made the point forcefully that illegal killing, e.g. the shooting or poisoning of raptors, 'tarnishes the whole reputation of game interests' and that it was one of his objectives to work 'with shooting interests to root out the small number of bad apples' engaged in illegal killing. Again I am in full agreement with that and the NGO does not tolerate illegal acts by any keeper. Clearly it is a very sensitive issue and Martin emphasised that illegal killing makes co-operation with shooting interests much more difficult for the RSPB. I completely respect and accept that point. There seem to be many areas of common ground between the RSPB and our world and I am sure that by talking more often we can better understand each other, which has to be to the benefit of the countryside as a whole.

Less positive have been recent (and I must say in my view sometimes ridiculous) utterances from Natural England. Back in 2005, Natural England's predecessor, English Nature, became involved in the consultation on licences for pest control, including the 'open' licence that allows for the control of wood pigeon.

English Nature proposed that anyone making use of the licence should demonstrate that they had tried non-lethal methods, such as scaring, before resorting to the shotgun. At the time the proposal drew ridicule and was unsurprisingly dropped, with common sense for once prevailing. Those involved in the control of pigeons were left to 'satisfy' themselves that the shooting of them was necessary: with an estimated 10,000,000 pigeons causing millions of pounds' worth of damage to agricultural crops each year in the UK, that is not exactly difficult.

Incredibly, Natural England has now decided to return to the debate. Another consultation has been launched with the inane slogan of 'shoo before you shoot'. Their suggestion is that farmers should take 'reasonable and appropriate steps, such as scaring' before shooting pigeons. In making such comments Natural England has not only made itself look somewhat ridiculous and out of touch, it has also demonstrated a complete lack of understanding of the central point, in that scaring away does not stop pigeons eating crops, it just moves them on to another farmer's fields. The problem is not solved by scaring, just relocated. In addition, Natural England is attempting to get such pests as crows, jackdaws and jays removed from the general (open) licence, which further demonstrates a complete lack of any grasp of reality in relation to the countryside.

The issue of pest control is one that does not endear the shooting world to its critics, but it is something that, as a gamekeeper, I would argue can be very important. Reactions can also be blown out of all proportion. Foxes and buzzards are our biggest concern. Whilst there is little we can do about the buzzard population, due to its legal protection, we can deter the birds from congregating around the pens. I would argue that shooting has actually increased the buzzard population by providing it with a ready source of food in terms of young, weak or wounded game birds. Personally I am not too obsessed with losses to buzzards, for it is very rare for them to take a healthy poult and I regard them as performing a useful service by removing sickly birds from the pens. The stress they cause can be an issue though, in that the mere presence of a buzzard near a pen can cause the birds inside to become nervous and this disrupts their feeding. Thus we do try to discourage buzzards from settling anywhere near the pens. During the shooting season these birds are a very common sight in the skies over Castle Hill, but it is noticeable that as soon as the season is over, and their immediate food source has gone, the buzzards move on.

I was intrigued to read in *The Field* of November 2013 that the RSPB itself actively applies predator control over its 130,000-hectare landholding. In 2011-12 its staff dispatched 241 foxes, 77 mink, 292 crows and 11 magpies, as well as numerous rats and grey squirrels. It even culled 600 deer, which, together with the species mentioned above, were controlled for the greater welfare of the flora and fauna on its land. Whilst the RSPB recognises that predator control is sometimes vital, it will always try to use non-lethal methods before resorting to a lethal approach. It may be considered that this is a worthy attitude but it can lead to undesirable results. For example, the use of expensive fox-proof fencing also restricts the free movement of other wild mammals. The area of predator control is a prime example of one in which this organisation might perhaps consider a more open and direct approach for the benefit of all our wildlife.

We work closely with local hunts to control foxes and of course do our best to keep the population down, especially near the pens. In younger days I actively controlled foxes all year round, but as I have slowed down slightly I now only target them during the first weeks after the poults have arrived, when the birds are at their most vulnerable. I have learnt that simply deterring a fox is much less work and anyway if a fox is shot or snared all we find is that another fox moves in to take over the vacant territory. We do electrify the release pens and also the ground outside, where a few young birds like to fly in the first month until they can fly up to roost. This decision has, I believe, saved us literally thousands of birds over the years from becoming fox food. We also place electric fencing around some of the more important cover crop areas to deter deer from destroying our hard work.

As in most things in life, there are usually unforeseen consequences of any action. In my experience this is never truer than when folk who don't really understand the countryside try to dictate or interfere from afar, usually for what they consider to be good reasons. The ban on stag-hunting on Exmoor is a classic case in point. I think most folk who became involved in the debate had no idea what happened on a stag hunt. Images of deer being ripped apart by hounds are probably what many had in their minds. This simply was not the case. The hounds were there to exhaust the stag in the chase and then to 'bring it to bay', in which the stag would be encircled by the barking hounds, thus allowing for the animal to be humanely killed. Before the ban, stag-hunting with hounds was a long established tradition on Exmoor. Farmers and landowners would frequently take part in the pursuit and were happy to allow the hounds across their land, especially at times when the population was such that the deer were causing damage to crops and trees.

Since the ban, the deer population has really begun to suffer. Exmoor does not offer the huge expanse of land with which the Scottish Highlands are blessed and deer have to compete with man to a much greater extent. In the past, the self-interest of hunting meant that the population was tolerated, but now it has to be managed almost as a kindness and this is not always the case. In frustration at the amount of damage being done to crops, and perhaps with an eye to financial gain, more rifles are being allowed on farmers' land and more deer are being shot. Of course, it is the healthy, trophy animals, rather than the sickly or weak specimens that the hounds would most likely have claimed, that are now being shot. Thus not only are numbers in a spiral of decline but the gene pool is being weakened too. It is critical that some sort of programme of management is considered, and considered quickly, or else the magnificent Exmoor stag will be lost to future generations. I am sure this is not what those who campaigned for the stag-hunting ban had in mind when they forced others to accept their will, but, as I say, this is a classic example of ill-informed do-gooders acting without proper forethought.

Every organisation, including BASC, the NGO or the RSPB, and every individual who has a love of the countryside, must not let their views be based on ill-founded emotions. For all our futures, it is vital that policies and practices are firmly centred on scientific work. If not, the countryside we all love and the flora and fauna that we are privileged to see and enjoy will be lost to us in a couple of generations. *The State of Nature* report has made this very clear. Time is not on our side.

Returning to the positive role that game-shooting and management can have on our fauna and flora, I would like to focus on the fact that on land where shooting is permitted, there is clear evidence to show that wildlife is more diverse and abundant. For example, the shooting community needs to demonstrate that our sport really does benefit the wild songbird population, as I have already explained. If we can do this as a start then maybe we can lead the way in bringing back some of the good things that have been lost in the countryside. I believe many shoots, and particularly Castle Hill, become a massive bird-table during and beyond the season as we ensure a food source at a time when nature is not so readily abundant. After the end of the 2013-14 season I was out early one morning and visited a patch of five or six acres of wildbird mix planted on the Brayley drive and there must have been what seemed like a thousand birds feeding on it. Literally a cloud of linnets, tits of all sorts, finches and sparrows took off as I approached: it was a wonderful sight to behold.

Through an initiative by both the Exmoor National Parks Authority and GESA it is hoped that a project can be launched in the not too distant future with the Game & Wildlife Conservation

Trust (GWCT). Their Chief Executive, Teresa Dent, is keen to do a survey on Exmoor of six woods on shoots which have a good habitat for wildlife and where pheasants are released in significant numbers, as well as looking at six additional woodland locations on Exmoor which are away from pheasant shoots. This will allow the GWCT to produce a 'compare and contrast' survey of the range of species of wildlife found in each location. This has never been done before and it is hoped that the results will scientifically demonstrate something those of us who work so close to the land already know to be a truth: that the plentiful food to be found on shooting ground means that wildlife is more varied and abundant than on land which has no association with shooting. The cost for the survey is to be in the region of £35,000 and we are looking to Exmoor shoots to part-fund it themselves, as well as fund-raise, so that this important survey can take place. It is hoped that the British Trust for Ornithology and the Forestry Commission will also come on board and perhaps help financially. This seems to me to be an ideal survey, the type that Natural England should be encouraging and assisting in, rather than focusing its attention on such things as changes to the general shotgun licence. It is likely that this survey will produce strong scientific support for the positive effects of shooting land management, and I think those involved should be encouraged by some sort of financial incentive to plant more wild-bird-mix cover crops.

In 2011 the NGO conducted a similar survey, entitled *Gamekeepers and Wildlife*. Of the 941 shoots that responded to the survey, fifty-nine per cent of them already planted wild bird and conservation mixtures as cover crops. The area of ground covered by the survey was in excess of 1,300,000 hectares – an area five times that of the National Nature Reserves (NNRs) designated in the United Kingdom and over thirteen times greater than the area covered by RSPB reserves. At just under sixty per cent of the total area covered by United Kingdom National Parks (2,245,394 hectares), by any measure this NGO survey was a substantial document. The primary purpose of the survey was to assess the quarry, predator and wildlife species found on shooting estates across the United Kingdom. Not only did the survey demonstrate the important role shooting plays in wildlife conservation but it also clearly showed that raptors are far more plentiful on land that is shot over than land that is not. I do hope that more independent studies, with greater numbers of respected bodies involved, will put an end to a lot of arguments by confirming that shooting is nothing but beneficial to the diversity and range of British wildlife. Such an outcome will be of real scientific interest and importance in itself.

The decline in the rabbit population in the past fifty years, largely as a result of that dreadful disease myxomatosis, has meant that predators, whether winged or footed, have been forced to look elsewhere for their food source. I personally think that this factor is an important one when considering the decline in our bird life and small mammal numbers. I must admit I do get rather angry when I hear well-meaning folk wanting to see the reintroduction of the pine marten or the goshawk, both of which are killing machines. These folk are basing their arguments on a type of countryside that is long gone, and with it the large rabbit population. Predators (especially those that may be reintroduced without a proper consideration of the countryside ecosystem as a whole) place a huge strain upon our existing small mammals and will continue to do so. Perhaps on Exmoor, and elsewhere, the pheasant has to some extent taken the place of the rabbit in the food chain and thus their presence is of huge benefit to wild life as a whole: the meat they provide has helped to fill the gap left by declining rabbit numbers.

Finally, I would just like to consider, perhaps rather selfishly, what I believe to be a serious threat to our sport. If it comes to pass, it will not only threaten livelihoods but will have a huge impact upon the countryside in general. This is the potential ban on lead shot in cartridges. Down in the West Country, where the stunning topography gives us the ability to show really high pheasants, there is simply no viable alternative to lead shot as yet. It is the most effective medium for killing high pheasants. A ban would not only result in more pricked birds, and thus more suffering, but it would also really threaten, if not totally jeopardise, the high bird shooting which is so important to the economy of the south-west, as I have demonstrated. This potential ban is another classic example of folk not fully understanding the consequences of their actions. I for one will not only fight a ban with all my strength, but I will also work tirelessly to try to find an alternative medium that works as effectively as lead shot. Until one is found, it would be wrong and dangerously inappropriate to ban lead shot.

I was recently asked the question – for a magazine article – that if I had the chance to change one aspect of game shooting in Britain, what would it be? Many ideas crossed my mind, ranging from the silly to the unrealistic, but one that stayed fixed would be to alter the dates of the pheasant shooting season. Our current dates of 1st October to 1st February have been with us for years and years and I think were established for good historical reasons, based on the shooting of wild birds and the use of broody hens. Things have, of course, moved on and I sincerely believe that we should consider a change to our current dates. I would personally advocate a move to see the season starting in mid-October and continuing until mid-February. Not only would the birds be stronger in the early weeks of the season but those surviving to the end of it would offer even more of a challenge than they do today. Such a move would also give keepers more flexibility in the rearing and release of birds, for our wet summers, which seem to be becoming such a feature, can cause real problems. If disease does become an issue at this time, the birds will have more time to recover. In addition the extra hours of daylight at the end of the season would be of real benefit.

I cannot deny that legacy is important to me. I also like to believe that everyone out there is a friend and I have always worked on this premise; the friendship of folk has been an important part of my life. In addition, I believe that you should work hard to improve on what you have got throughout life. I would like to be remembered as someone who has improved things and that my time at Castle Hill has been well spent. I take great pleasure today when I drive around the Estate and see trees I have planted that are now mature, adding to a good drive and making it a great one. I would like to think in years to come that when folk are beating or shooting at Kite's Nest, they might remember that Brian Mitchell was responsible for the drive and if they did, it would give me huge pleasure. I am thrilled that many of the keepers who have worked with me are still fully employed within the industry, the majority now as Head Keepers in their own right. I am delighted that during my career I have been able to make a contribution to the world of shooting, and, particularly important to me, improvements in pheasant welfare. I know that my name is often associated with the development of high bird shooting on Exmoor, particularly at Miltons and in North Devon at Castle Hill, but I know, too, that for all the work I have put in over the years, nothing would have been achieved without the help, support and vision of gentlemen like Alan Milton and Caspar MacDonald-Hall. I owe them, and so many others, a huge debt of gratitude.

When I began my gamekeeping career, my father took some delight in telling me that there was no future in such work. He was wrong about that then, but whether he might be proved right in the next generation is up to all of us involved in shooting now. We must make sure we act responsibly, consider our environment and defend shooting with passion and determination, to make sure that our sport continues for centuries to come. Shooting will always be under attack by some good folk who have a dislike of it and perhaps an incorrect perception of what it is all about. For all the pleasure shooting has given me and millions of others, it is our duty continually to educate, defend our sport and show a willingness to get youngsters involved in it and in our countryside.

If I can inspire others to do this, I would regard it as my most important legacy and one in which I would take greatest pride.

I do pity the person who takes on my responsibilities once I finally retire, not because I think I will be a hard act to follow (I am no Sir Alex Ferguson!) but because I know I will find it hard not to interfere or offer my opinion, whether it is wanted or not. However, I also know that I will have to move on and resist that temptation. I will say here and now that when I finally get to meet the Great Head Keeper in the sky, and my bones are resting in the churchyard overlooking Castle Hill, whoever is Head Keeper should know that I will be taking a very keen interest in how each shoot day is going. If a loud 'tutting' noise is heard or a shout of 'Fiver!' in the wind, then I might be closer than folk think.

I would like to end my story and my thoughts (for what they are worth) with one of Gillian Tredgold's wonderful poems, which captures the feeling that I have at the end of one season and the expectation of the next. Long may I be privileged to go out on shoot days myself, and I sincerely hope that future generations are able, and are allowed, both to enjoy the wonderful sport of shooting and our lovely, inspiring countryside.

Silence

The woods are silent now
The last gun is still
No whistle is heard for retrieving dogs
No keeper's cry so shrill

Range Rovers are gone from the track,
With their rich food, cigars and champagne,
The trees are quietly watching now
In the gently falling rain

A fox peeps out from behind a fir
To see if the coast is clear,
There's nothing now to disturb his peace –
Only an owl or a deer.

A buzzard circles overhead,
Utters his plaintive cry,
He spies no men with dogs and guns
As he soars across the sky.

But the woods are only resting
Until autumn comes round again,
And the pheasants take flight and we don our Barbours
For more fun on shoot days in the rain!

POSTSCRIPT

Whilst researching this book I have spoken to numerous folk who have known and worked with Brian Mitchell over the years. Many had very nice things to say about the man, but the inclusion of their comments within the text would not really have followed the narrative. Consequently, I have decided (without telling Brian, for as a modest man he will hate this particular section) to record a few of their remarks. These words describe Brian better than any writer could.

'Brian is an absolute perfectionist. He likes to challenge himself at the end of every season to look at ways to improve the shoot, with improvements to existing drives or to the consideration of introducing new ones. That approach keeps Castle Hill fresh and exciting. There is never a single day's shooting at Castle Hill in which Brian does not do the very best he can for whoever is shooting. Brian is a great egalitarian who favours no one, but simply wishes for all to enjoy their time at Castle Hill. Brian is terribly community-minded and has done so much for the local community. He is also very loyal, both to the shoot and those who live and work on the Estate and nearby. He is a huge giver and a formidable man.'

Caspar MacDonald-Hall, Castle Hill

'Brian was the first; he set the benchmark that every up-and-coming keeper and beat-keeper aspires to.'

Peter Baxendale

'Brian is unique in the world of shooting and his ideas have transformed the world of gamekeeping. Brian understands nature; he thinks like a bird. He is an extraordinary man, a very likeable man and a very kind man.'

Lady Arran

'Brian is a real ambassador for shooting; thoughtful and wise.'

Dr Nigel Stone, Exmoor National Park Authority

'Brian has been, and remains, a mover and shaker within the world of shooting and I have huge respect for the man.'

Dan Reynolds, Roxtons

'A great many people, myself included, owe Brian and Alan Milton a great deal for pioneering Exmoor shoots which have contributed hugely to the local economy. Brian and Alan were revolutionaries and their energy and enthusiasm has not only transformed Exmoor but shooting nationally.'

Sir Edward Goschen

'Brian has always been kind and supportive of me and generous with his time. Nothing is too much trouble. He is a remarkable man with very great qualities.'

Angus Barnes, Loyton Shooting Group

'Brian has always been someone to get involved and take responsibility for the profession for which he is so passionate. He does this with good humour and a twinkle in his eye.'

Teresa Dent, Chief Executive
Game & Wildlife Conservation Trust

'It is a privilege to know Brian, and to be able to count him as a friend. His determination and dedication are at the centre of his success.'

Hugh Thomas, Land Agent

'Brian is at one with nature. He is a man for everybody; kind and generous.'

Valerie Woulf, Shoot Syndicate Administrator

'Brian's longevity at Castle Hill is a huge testament to him. He is still on top of his game and always looking forward.'

Paul Smalley, Estate Manager, Castle Hill

'Brian can be stubborn. His dedication to the sport, and the welfare of birds, is total. He is always looking ahead, never resting on his laurels. Brian can be difficult, but he has an annoying habit of usually being right. Simply, he is an inspiration.'

Alan Beynon, Vet

'Brian is quite simply a magician. If there was an Olympics for game shooting it would be held at Castle Hill. Over the last ten years it has been about shooting that higher bird consistently and Castle Hill is the pinnacle of that. I shoot some seventy-plus days all over the UK and I keep coming back to the best, Castle Hill. Brian is like wine; you can go all over the world tasting the fruits of other continents only to return to left bank Bordeaux with a south-west wind blowing up its ass!'

Simon Ford, businessman and regular gun at Castle Hill

'Brian is able to play the tune on a shoot day and he seems to know where the pheasants will fly before even they do. He is relentless in his dedication and passion to his profession. He never rests on his laurels, and is never satisfied. He is always looking to improve Castle Hill and develop the people he works with. Brian, with his years of experience and accumulated knowledge has become something of a guru, and a modest one at that.

On a day when I am standing in the line on, say, the Deer Park, Colythorn or Brayley, and the exceptional Castle Hill birds begin to come over, I know there is nowhere in the world I would rather be, for Castle Hill is simply the best shoot in the world and that fact is down to the commitment and skill Brian possesses and his strong relationship with Caspar.'

Bob Sperring, regular gun at Castle Hill

'Brian is very focused on legacy and wants Castle Hill to be as good, if not better, a shoot in forty years' time as it is now. He is thinking of the future all the time and to how drives will perform and improve over the years. It is a shame Brian is so ugly and so crap in bed. I would trust Brian with anything...apart from my wife!'

Peter Gould, friend and loader at Castle Hill

'Brian is unique; a perfectionist.'

David Sexon, shooting instructor and loader

'Brian is a forward thinker who is never afraid to make the big call.'

Phil Lay, loader

'Brian is totally reliable; he is always there for his friends and will make time for them even when he is so very busy.'

Alan Sexon, loader and driver

INDEX

Ali, Richard 144
Alnwick Park shoot 146
Alresford, Lord 149
Arran, Lady 74, 78, 82, 88, 106, 112, 208
Atkins, June 35
Atkinson, Mark 65-6, 82, 104-5

Ball, Tony 58, 67
Barnes, Angus 134, 154, 159, 170-7, 209
Bartlett, Bert and John 83
Barnstaple 38-9, 68-9
Baxendale, Johnny 74
Baxendale, Peter 71, 103-4, 106, 208
Beavis, Ivor 145
Bennett, Richard 190-1
Benson, Helen 149
Berghmans, Baron Jean-Pierre 130
Bernhard,
    HRH Prince of the Netherlands 58
Best, Admiral 29
Beynon, Alan 122-8, 130, 133, 154, 176, 193-4, 209
Blackmoor Gate 66
Boconnoc Estate 11
Boniface, Nick 66-7
Botham, Ian 58
Bradley shoot 159, 183
Bridgetown CC 44-5, 57
Brimacombe, Nigel, Marion,
    Paul and Claire 77
Brine, Alex 91
British Association for Shooting and Conservation (BASC) 141, 144-7, 149, 156, 190, 195, 201
British Trust for Ornithology 161, 202
Brooks, John 66, 132
Broome, David 58
Brown, Ben 153, 157
Brown, George 33, 64
Brown, Nigel 34-5
Buccleuch shoot 130
Buckleigh, Mike 86
Buckmaster, Henry 34
'bulgy eye' disease 125
Bulland shoot 43, 65-70, 82, 132, 164
Buttery shoot 183

Cannon, Stuart 146
Carlisle, Gordon 51-2
Carter, Charlie 27
Castle Hill 8-10, 12, 17-19, 25, 46-7, 51, 69, 72-5, 77, 80-2, 86-7, 90-3, 95-107, 110, 118, 130-6, 151, 169-170, 176-9, 182, 188-190, 193, 199, 201, 205-6, 208-210
    challenging birds 64-5, 76-82, 142-3, 177-9, 182, 188-90
    cover crops 111-4, 116
    density of birds 120
    feed 157
    fibre and plastic wads 138-141
    forestry 106-111
    house days 103-104
    managing the day 90-102
    new drives 83-9
    offered position of Head Keeper 69-75
    poaching 104-5
    quality of birds 138, 141-3, 151-5
    rabbit trappers 22
    release pens 119-122, 128, 154
    rearing of birds 121, 125-6, 128-9, 151-155
    song bird population 25, 161, 201
    wind direction 112
Cawthorne, Dick 82
Challacombe shoot 66, 134, 175
    establishment of 131-3
Chargot shoot 43, 65-7, 69, 80, 90, 153, 155, 164, 182
Chandris, John 70, 81
Chandris, Michael 70, 81

Church, Charles 67, 69, 71
Clapworthy, Robert 59
Clark, David 13, 130, 145-6
Coccidiosis 121, 128
Combe Sydenham shoot 134, 171-2, 174
Conachie, Mike 172
Conachie, Pete 171-2
Cook, John 86
Countryside Alliance 178
Cricket 11, 26
  on Exmoor 44, 45, 47, 57-9, 154, 187

Day, Ron 25, 27, 29-31
De Rusett, Gareth 91
Deer 27, 30, 37, 79-80, 105, 162, 188, 199-200, 207
Deer Park Side shoot 27
Dent, Teresa 202, 209
Devon Air Ambulance 178, 181
Digweed, George 172
Doubleday, Nelson, Jr 55, 58
Down, Andrew 83

Edgcott shoot 175
Eggins, Robert 179
Elliot, Alan 81
English Heritage 112
English Nature 197-8
Exeter 122, 147, 187
Exmoor 9, 36-7, 58, 68, 70-1, 73, 83, 120-1, 123, 125, 127, 131, 133, 161, 163, 167, 202-3
  Buying Group 157-9, 175
  early life on Exmoor 39-49
  Greater Exmoor Shoots Association (GESA) 166-9, 175, 183, 201
  National Park 163-9, 201, 209
  shooting and the Exmoor high bird 49-51, 53-5, 57-9, 63, 65, 71, 134-5, 138, 140-1, 143, 149, 150, 154, 160, 164, 168, 170, 171-9, 182-4, 189-190, 192, 205, 209
  stag hunting 200
Exmoor Keepers' Challenge 160

Facey, Alec 86
Fieldsend, Malcolm 146-7
Filleigh 86, 178
Firth, Mark 67
Ford, Simon 99, 210
Fortescue family 106
Fortescue, Lady Margaret 74, 82, 106
Fox, foxes, fox hunting 22-4, 28, 33-5, 43, 59, 79-80, 102, 105, 129, 131-2, 168, 181, 195, 199-200, 207
Fryer, Bob 46
Fussell, Phil 58

Game & Wildlife Conservation Trust (GWCT) 161, 178, 201-2, 209
Game farms 122-6, 151-6
Game Finders 37-8
Gamekeepers' Welfare Trust 145, 149, 179, 182
Goodchild, David 64
Goschen, Sir Edward 55, 164, 171, 209
Gould, Peter 46, 56, 77, 97, 100-1, 179, 210
Greenham, Tom 54
Grintow, Keith 36-7, 46
Gurston Down shoot 50, 62

Haddeo shoot 134, 159, 171, 175, 178-9, 183
Hardwick Game Farm 153, 157
Harper, Martin 194, 197
Hawkins, Janet 58
Hayes, Mike 44
Head, John 27
Heath Fritillary Butterfly 167
Hedges, Mark 147
Hembury, Phil 157
Henstridge, Arthur 24
Hewitt, Peter 80
Hexamita meleagridis 123-4
Hitchings, David 50
Hoare, Tim 102
Hogan, Paul 59-62
Hollam shoot 183

Honeycombe shoot 27
Hunter, Bob 159, 183
Hunting 43-4, 49, 59, 131-2, 196
Hunting Act 2004 181
stag hunting 168, 200-1
Hussell, Tania 178

Jenkins, Richard 66-7
Joyce, Bill 58, 64

Kirby, Chris 183
Kirkland, David 55-6
Knight, Ron 23-4, 33, 131

Lapsley, Jack (and Hopey) 55, 57-8
Latham, Brian 87
Laurels 88, 114-5, 127
Lay, Phil 97, 100-2, 210
League Against Cruel Sports 169-170
Liddle, Gary 80
Liscombe shoot 183
Lichfield, Patrick, Earl of 58
Littlecott Estate 53
Loyton shoot 159, 171
Loyton Shooting Group 134, 154, 170-6, 182, 209

MacDonald-Hall, Caspar 70-1, 81-2, 87, 132, 135, 143, 172, 178, 205, 208, 210
MacDonald-Hall, Sam, Commander 69-71, 74-6, 81-2
Macleod, Graham 87
Maize 62-3, 67, 88-9, 112-6, 118-9, 162
Malet, Sir Edward 66
Malet, Harry 66
Mann, Alan 54
Mapperton 31-9, 42, 46, 64, 104
MacFarlane Game Farm 152-3
Marshall, John 153
Melcombe shoot 183
Michael, HRH Prince, of Kent 58
Milborne Port 20-22, 24
Milton, Alan
at Miltons 40-2, 50-1, 53-5, 62, 64-9, 138
pioneer 209
relaxed approach 75
roving syndicate 38-9
shooting at Mapperton 33
supportive 205
Temple shoot 82
Miltons 9, 11-2, 37, 39-44, 46-52, 55-71, 73, 77-8, 82, 90, 112, 138, 151, 159, 164, 174, 178, 182-3, 205
commercial shooting 53-4
expansion 65-7
leaving Miltons 68-71, 73
naming of drives 64
Miscanthus grass 88, 113, 115-6
Mitchell, Anna 41
Mitchell, Angie 5, 8-9, 11, 13, 18, 35, 70-1, 73, 77, 142, 163
Mitchell, Lisa 58
Mitchell, Robert 41, 46, 49, 66-7, 80-1, 141, 154, 156, 160, 168, 170, 179
Mitchell, Sally 32-3, 40-1, 48-9, 54, 56-8, 70
Mitchell, Simon 41,46
Molland 180
Moore, David 71
Mornacott shoot 183
Musto, Ian 99
Myxomatosis 21, 203

National Gamekeepers' Organisation (NGO) 12, 16-7, 126, 130, 144, 156, 165, 179, 181, 186, 190
formation of the NGO 147-9
Gamekeepers and Wildlife 202
NGO and the RSPB 195, 197, 201
Natural England 197-8, 202
North Molton shoot 66-7, 81, 87, 141, 154, 159, 170-1, 178
Northcote, Ed 91

Oliver, Chris 37-8
Orssich, Chris 53-4, 56-7, 67
Oscroft, Terry 146

Partridge, grey 22, 24, 63
red-legged 62

Pearce, Maurice 12
Perrin, Alan 97
Peterborough Game 190
Phillips, Captain Mark 58
Phytophthora ramorum 108-9
Poaching 104-5
Potter, Steve 69

Rackenford shoot 46
Rawlence, Michael 74
Reed, John 45
Reynolds, Dan 67, 140, 159, 209
Reynolds, Martin 64
Riprand von Arco, Count 129-130
Rivkin, Michael 69-70, 81
Roberts, Kevin 158
Roff, Tony 149
Roxburghe, Duke of 58
Roxtons sporting agency 53-6, 58, 65, 67, 138, 140, 209
Royal Society for the Protection of Birds (RSPB) 161, 194-7, 199, 201-2

Sandwich, Earl of, (Victor Montagu) 31-3, 35, 38-9
Sefton, Alan 146
Sexon, Alan 83, 86, 97, 135, 210
Sexon, David 100-102, 192, 210
Sherborne Castle Estate 25, 28-32, 58, 104, 130
Sherborne, Dorset 25
Sherring, Doug 44
Shooting Gazette 150
Shooting Times 51, 53, 147
Simonsbath 66
Smalley, Paul 107, 109-112, 209
Snell, George 83
Sparsholt College 192
Sperring, Bob 182, 210
Sporting Gun 64
Stags, stag hounds, stag hunting 43, 118, 168, 180, 185-6, 200-1
Stevens, Charles 56
Stone, Dr Nigel 165, 208
Stuckeridge shoot 134, 175
Stucley, George 170
Sturdza, Prince Eric 6, 10, 102
Swain, Ernie 28
Swift, John 144, 146

Tawstock shoot 135
Temple shoot 74-5, 77, 82-3, 104, 106-7
The Field 139, 199
The State of Nature report 195-6, 201
Thomas, Hugh 78-9, 82-3, 85, 107, 132, 166, 209
Thomas-Everard, Christopher 39, 43, 48, 60
Tredgold, Gillian
    poems 8, 207
    Rules for Beaters 118
Turner, Brian 46, 77
Turner, John 27-9

Utopia cover crop 113-4

Velcourt 110

Waddell, Lindsay 148
Walker, Stuart 91
Wallace, Captain Ronnie 131-2
Wellshead shoot 159, 183
West London Shooting School 179
West Molland shoot 66, 164, 170
Westcott, Tom 47
Westermill shoot 183
Westminster, Duke of 58
Whitby, Dave 146
Wild bird mix 113, 116, 161, 202
Winsford 48, 56
Witheridge, George 180
Withycombe shoot 182
Withypool 49
Wiveliscombe 65, 160
Woolland shoot 22, 24
Wood, Giles 34-5, 46
Wood Advent shoot 183
Woulf, Valerie 82, 209

Yandle, John 27
Yardley, Mike 139
Yeo, Danny 105

Other books by Stephen Manning

Non-fiction

Evelyn Wood VC, Pillar of Empire
Soldiers of the Queen
Quebec – The Story of Three Sieges – A Military History
The Martini-Henry Rifle
It Was Never My Ambition to Become a Hooker

Fiction

Thorverton and the Nile

Contributor

Victoria's Generals Edited by Ian Beckett

www.stephen-manning.co.uk/author